Modern Sewing Projects

compiled by **Lindsey Murray McClelland**

© 2013 Interweave Press LLC
All rights reserved.

Interweave grants permission to photocopy the templates in this publication for personal use.

The projects in this collection were originally published in other Interweave publications, including 101 Patchwork, Modern Patchwork, Quilt Scene, Quilting Arts, *and* Stitch *magazines and 'QATV.' Some have been altered to update information and/or conform to space limitations.*

Interweave Press LLC
A division of F+W Media, Inc
201 East Fourth Street
Loveland, CO 80537
interweave.com

Manufactured in the United States by Versa Press

ISBN 978-1-59668-768-4 (pbk.)

Table of Contents

4 **Fabric Bottle Bud Vase**
Lucie Summers

6 **Marbles Table Runner**
Brigitte Heitland

9 **Black & White Place Mats**
Alissa Haight Carlton

11 **Patchwork Cube Slipcover**
Kevin Kosbab

14 **Cable Clutter Cleanup Bags**
Kathy York

16 **Color Swatch Wall Hanging**
Sheryl Schleicher

19 Fabric Birds
Terry Grant

23 Rubik's Crush
Ashley Newcomb

25 Reusable Produce Bags
Lisa Chin

26 Travel Lingerie Bag
Blair Stocker

30 Alphabet Baby Quilt
Erin Gilday

35 Yoga Mat Carrier
Vivika Hansen DeNegre

37 Plastic Bag Dispenser
Ayumi Takahashi

39 Cell Phone Case
Mary Claire Goodwin

41 Sweet & Simple Key Fob
Corinnea Martindale

42 Patchwork Fabric Cuffs
Lucie Summers

43 Sewing Basics

Materials
— Paper glue stick
— Bud Vase template on page 5
— Piece of card stock to make a template (a cereal box is fine)
— Assorted fabric scraps
— Heavyweight interfacing
— Spray basting glue
— Empty glass or plastic jam jar

Optional
— Embellishments (ribbons, silk threads, beads)
— Walking foot attachment

Directions

1 For a standard-sized jam jar, make a photocopy of the template. Using the glue stick, adhere the paper template to the cereal box and cut out. Put the template to one side until later.

2 Stitch the fabric scraps together. Don't worry about size or color; just keep stitching until you have enough patchwork to cover the template. Make 4 patchwork pieces this size.

3 On the heavyweight interfacing, draw around the template and cut out 4 times.

4 Use the basting spray to coat the back of each interfacing shape and stick them to the wrong side of the patchwork fabric pieces.

Caution: Remember to use the basting spray in a well-ventilated room!

5 Trim off the excess fabric. You should be left with 4 patchwork bottle shapes. If you are embellishing your vase, embroider, stitch, and sew on your beads now. Remember to keep all of the edges free of heavily beaded decoration so you can satin-stitch easily.

6 Put the walking foot attachment on your sewing machine (this is not completely necessary; it just stops the two pieces from sliding away from one another—a normal foot will work too). Using a satin stitch, stitch the bottle tops and bottoms so they are neat and tidy.

7 Pair up the bottle shapes. Pin the right-hand side of 1 pair and the left-hand side of the other. For both

Fabric Bottle BUD VASE
by Lucie Summers

My husband never seems to be able to throw his beer bottles in the recycle bin—and in a way it's a good thing as it was a row of his bottles that inspired this patchwork bud vase!

pairs, satin-stitch the sides of the bottle shapes together, going slowly and precisely.

8 Take 1 of the already stitched pieces and turn it inside out so the interfacing is facing outwards. Turn it around so you can see the patchwork fabric and place it inside the other piece, so the wrong sides are together. Line up the edges and pin.

9 Satin-stitch the third side. Go slowly near the bottle neck. It is not difficult to do, but it's the trickiest part as there is less room to maneuver.

10 Pin and stitch the fourth side of the vase. Place your hand up inside the bottle shape and pop it back into shape. Tie off all the loose ends and darn them in.

11 Fill the jam jar with water and place the bottle vase over the top. Place one or two blossoms into your new vase, ensuring the stems are in the water. Step back and enjoy!

Visit **LUCIE SUMMERS'S** website at summersville.etsy.com.

Tips

* If you are feeling confident, make up your own vase shape. It might be worth making a paper mock-up first to ensure all the pieces fit together.

* Remember, the sky is the limit. The patchwork can be embellished with beads, ribbons, embroidery—both hand and machine. Just remember to leave the sides free of heavy beading so you can stitch the shapes together.

* Each vase can be made to fit a theme or season. These would be beautiful for a simple wedding centerpiece or red-and-white as a gorgeous Christmas greenery display!

* Never forget the impact of having several vases grouped together on a mantel or window ledge. These would look fantastic lined up in a row with just one or two blooms in each, especially if each vase is a slightly different shape.

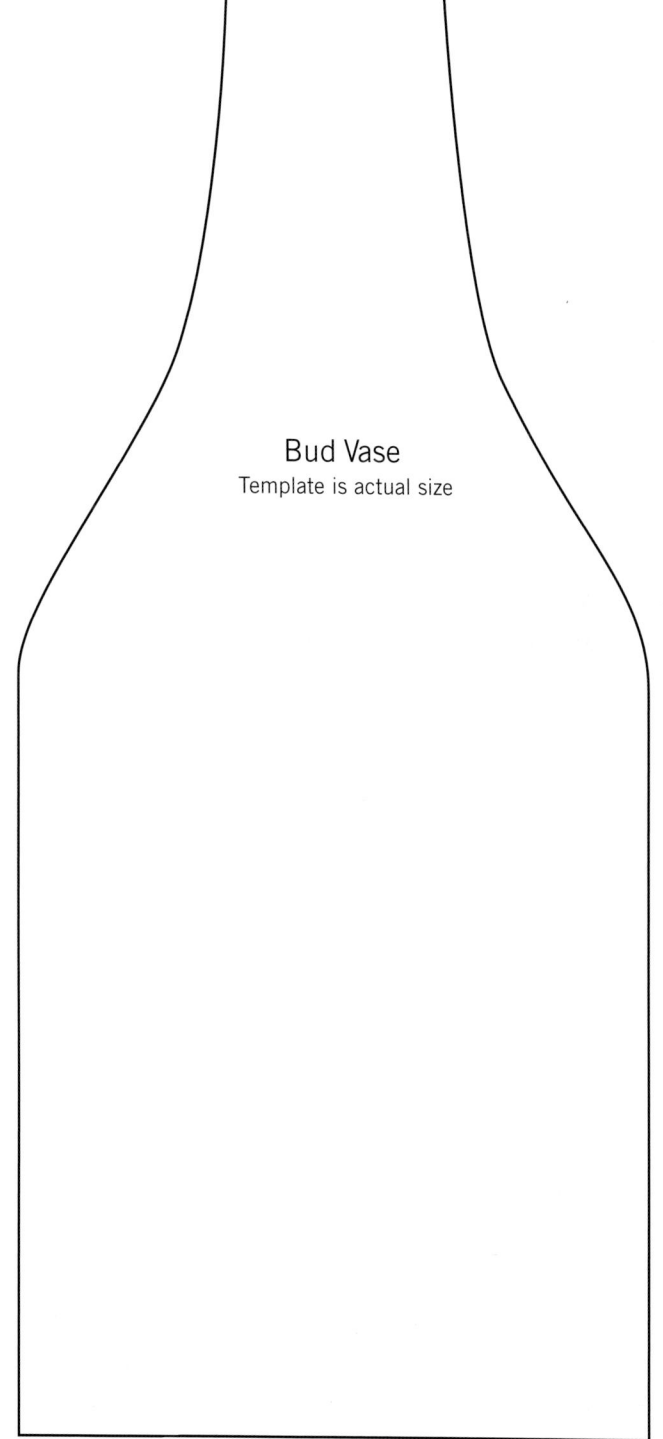

Bud Vase
Template is actual size

FABRIC BOTTLE BUD VASE 5

Marbles Table Runner
by Brigitte Heitland

Add a modern, sophisticated style to your table; let eyes be caught by colorful dots and some straight quilting lines. This machine-appliquéd table runner will make a splash in your dining room! The featured piece includes solid fabrics by Makower, and the printed fabrics are from my Juggling Summer fabric collection.

Materials

Note: All yardages are based on 44" (112 cm) wide fabric.

- Cream solid (background and backing), 1 yd (45.5 cm)
- Tan solid, 1 yd (45.5 cm)
- Assorted print scraps (I used fat sixteenths from 5 different print fabrics.)
- Batting, 32" × 16" (81.5 × 40.5 cm) piece (Use a thin cotton batting.)
- Freezer paper, 1 square yd (91.5 cm)
- Coordinating sewing and quilting threads
- Non-permanent marking tool
- Basting spray
- Templates on page 8

Finished Size
32" × 16" (81.5 × 40.5 cm)

note

✻ All seam allowances are ¼" (6 mm) unless otherwise stated. Please read carefully through all of the instructions before starting.

Directions

1 Enlarge the templates (provided) as indicated. Trace all of the patterns, without the seam allowances, onto the dull side of a sheet of freezer paper. Cut out the freezer paper templates.

2 Iron the shiny side of both freezer paper L-shaped templates onto the wrong side of the tan solid fabric, and iron the freezer paper circles onto the wrong side of the assorted prints. Leaving a ¼" (6 mm) seam allowance around each freezer paper shape, cut out all of the circles and the L's.

3 From the cream solid fabric cut 2 rectangles, each 32½" × 16½" (82.5 × 42 cm); set aside 1 rectangle for the backing.

Note: The L-shaped fabrics will be partially appliquéd to the background fabric (the outer portions of the L's will be caught in the seam allowance around the outside of the runner, so the outer edges need not be appliquéd).

4 To prepare the L-shaped fabrics for appliqué, clip into the seam allowance as marked on the pattern,

FIGURE 1

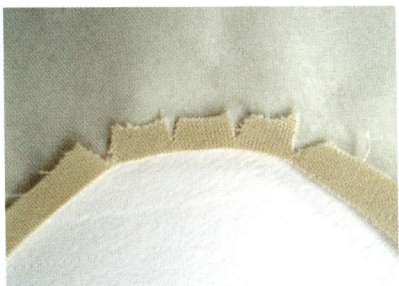

FIGURE 2

FIGURE 3

FIGURE 4

Process photos by Brigitte Heitland

clipping to within a thread of the freezer paper. Fold the edge of the fabric (just the portion that will be appliquéd over onto the freezer paper. Iron the folded edge to the freezer paper to hold it in place **(figure 1)**.

5 Clip the inside curves to within a thread of the seam allowance, to get the curves really smooth **(figure 2)**.

6 For the circles, sew a row of running stitches close to the edge of the fabric circle. Pull the running stitches carefully to gather up the edge of the fabric circle around the edge of the freezer paper. Press, creating a sharp folded edge.

7 Carefully pull out all of the freezer paper templates from the circles and the L's. Set aside the circles.

8 Position the L fabrics on the cream background and pin them in place. Using an invisible thread and your sewing machine's appliqué stitch, sew the turned part of the edges of the L's to the cream fabric. Leave the outer edges unfinished, so they match the raw edges of the cream background perfectly **(figure 3)**.

9 Cut the batting just a little bit smaller than the measurements of your finished table runner to avoid too much bulk at the edges. (I cut it 31¾" × 15¾" [80.5 × 40 cm].) Using the rounded corners of the L-shape patterns as a guide, round off the corners of your batting rectangle. Spray the batting with basting spray and center it on the wrong side of the appliquéd table runner front (or baste it).

10 With right sides together, layer the table runner top on the backing; pin or baste the edges. Stitch around the outside edge to sew the layers together, leaving an 8" (20.5 cm) opening (centered on 1 long side of the rectangle) and backstitching at each end. Clip the outside curves to within a thread of the seam allowance, to get your curves really smooth **(figure 4)**.

11 Turn the runner right-side out through the opening. Smooth the curves and carefully iron the runner flat. To close the opening, fold the seam allowance on each side of the opening in toward the wrong side. Then pin the opening closed and slipstitch by hand.

12 To quilt the runner as I did, on half of the front mark some horizontal, slightly diagonal lines; on the other half do the same in a vertical direction **(figure 5)**. Using a cream-colored thread, quilt on these lines. Vary the lines for a playful look.

13 Position the circles onto the runner and pin them in place **(figure 6)**.

14 Using a matching thread, slipstitch the circle appliqués in place by passing the needle through the folded edge of the appliqué and then through the background fabric. Proceed to blindstitch all around the shapes. Alternatively, if you prefer to machine-appliqué the circles in place, use an invisible thread and your sewing machine's appliqué stitch.

Congratulations! Your table runner is finished.

Visit **BRIGITTE HEITLAND'S** website at brigitteheitland.de.

FIGURE 5

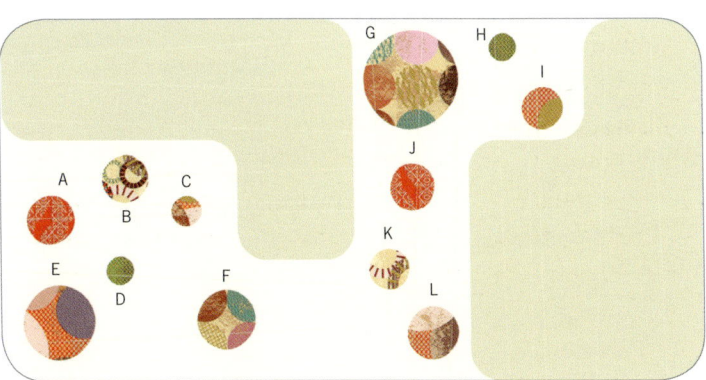

FIGURE 6

MARBLES TABLE RUNNER 7

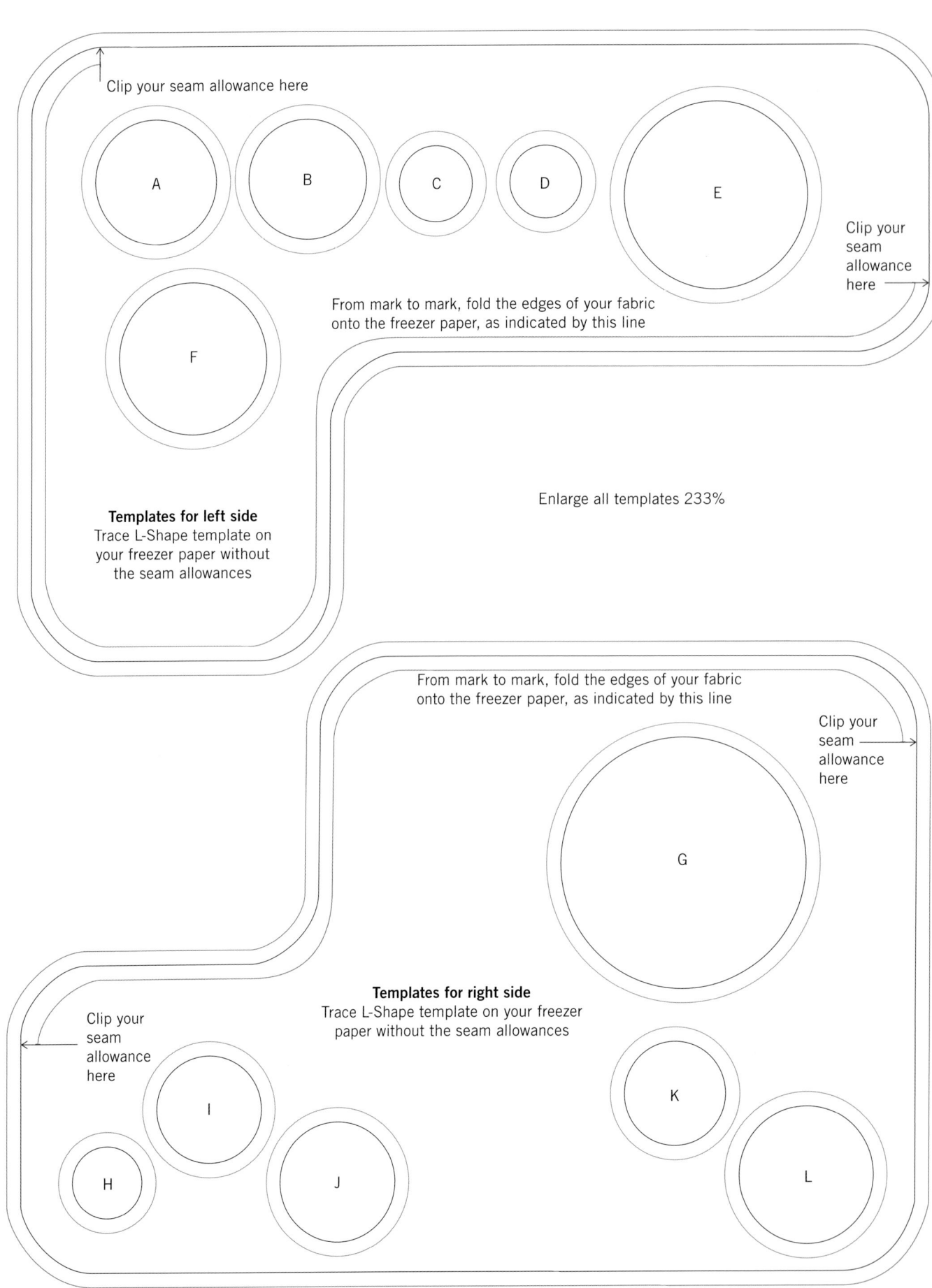

Materials
For one place mat

—Fabric A (white), ¼ yd (23 cm)

—Fabric B (black), ¼ yd (23 cm)

—Backing fabric, 1 fat quarter (22" × 18" [56 × 45.5 cm])

—Batting, 22" × 18" (56 × 45.5 cm) rectangle

—Binding fabric, ¼ yd (23 cm)

Finished Size
14" × 19" (35.5 × 48.5 cm)

notes

* The key to making sure these place mats fit is to cut out each piece the precise size and to stitch with an accurate (slightly scant) ¼" (6 mm) seam allowance. It is essential to carefully keep track of all of the pieces. As you cut out each piece be sure to pin a label to it so that you can keep track of all of the little different bits of fabric.

* If you are making more than one place mat, consider stacking your fabrics and cutting out all of the place mat pieces at once.

Cutting
See chart on page 10.

Assembling
Once you have cut out all of the pieces, you will assemble them as shown in **figures 1** and **2** on page 10. The place mat breaks down into four portions that, once assembled, are put together.

Upper left portion

1 Sew together A1, B1, A2 and A3, B3, A4. Sew these strips to either side of B2, and then sew A5 to the bottom. Add B4 to the right side and set aside.

2 Sew A7 to B6. Add A8 to the right side. Sew B5 to the top, and sew A6 to the left of your piecing. Add A9 to the top and B7 to the bottom.

3 Assemble A10, B8, A11, and sew to the bottom of your piecing. Sew this piecing to the right side of B4 (the unit that was set aside in Step 1). Set aside again.

Black & White Place Mats
by Alissa Haight Carlton

These graphic place mats add to any modern kitchen. Make them in any two contrasting colors for bold results.

Cutting Chart

Fabric A (white)

A1, A2, A3, A4 = 1½" × 4½"
A5 = 3" × 1½"
A6 = 1" × 3½"
A7 = 1" × 1"
A8 = 1½" × 3"
A9 = 2½" × 1½"
A10 = 1" × 5½"
A11 = 1½" × 5½"
A12 = 2" × 1½"
A13 = 2" × 3"
A14 = 2" × 5"
A15 = 3" × 1"
A16 = 3" × 1½"
A17 = 1½" × 1"
A18 = 1" × 1½"
A19 = 4½" × 1"
A20 = 4" × 1½"
A21 = 4" × 1"
A22 = 1½" × 3"
A23 = 1½" × 5½"
A24 = 2" × 3"
A25 = 2" × 4½"
A26 = 3" × 1½"
A27 = 2½" × 3"
A28 = 1½" × 1½"
A29 = 2" × 5½"
A30 = 2" × 9"
A31 = 1½" × 1"
A32 = 2" × 9"
A33 = 1½" × 1½"
A34 = 2" × 1½"
A35 = 6½" × 1½"
A36 = 1½" × 1½"
A37 = 1½" × 1"
A38 = 3" × 1½"
A39 = 5" × 1"
A40, A41, A42 = 2" × 3"

Fabric B (black)

B1 = 1½" × 1½"
B2 = 1" × 9½"
B3 = 1½" × 1½"
B4 = 1½" × 10½"
B5 = 2" × 1"
B6 = 1" × 2½"
B7 = 2½" × 1½"
B8 = 1" × 5½"
B9 = 1½" × 10½"
B10 = 2" × 1"
B11 = 2" × 1½"
B12 = 1" × 10½"
B13 = 19" × 2"
B14 = 1½" × 1"
B15 = 4½" × 1½"
B16 = 1" × 3"
B17 = 4" × 1½"
B18 = 1" × 3"
B19 = 1½" × 1½"
B20 = 1½" × 9"
B21 = 2" × 1½"
B22 = 1½" × 8"
B23 = 1½" × 1½"
B24 = 1" × 5½"
B25 = 1½" × 8½"
B26, B27 = 1½" × 1½"
B28 = 11" × 1"
B29 = 1½" × 1"
B30 = 5" × 1½"
B31 = 1" × 3"
B32 = 1½" × 3"

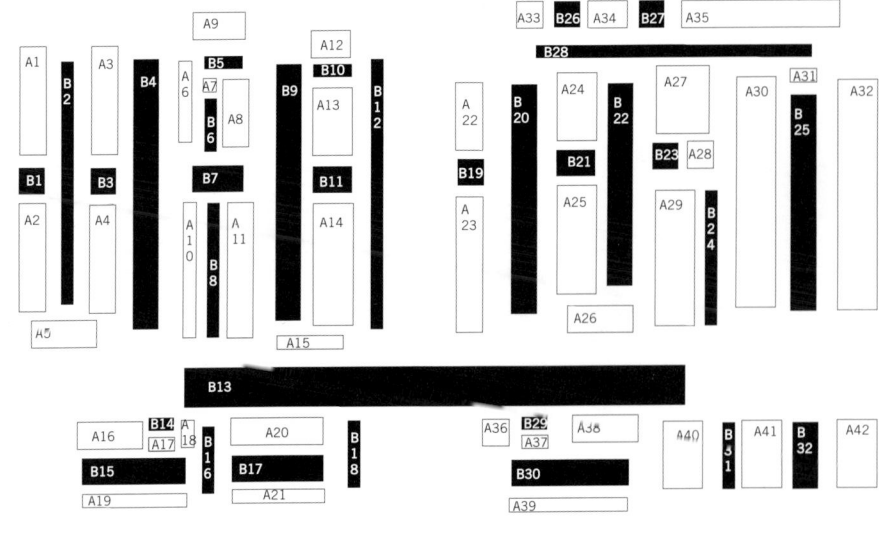
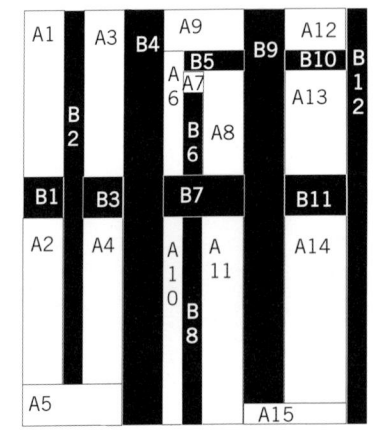
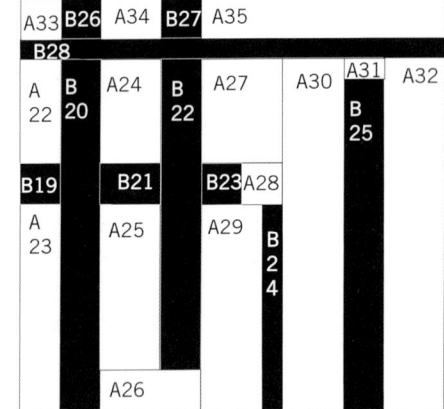

FIGURE 1

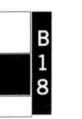

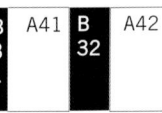

FIGURE 2

4 Working top to bottom, assemble A12, B10, A13, B11, A14. Sew B9 to the left side, add A15 to the bottom, and sew B12 to the right side of this piecing.

5 Finish the upper left portion by sewing this piecing to the right side of the piecing previously set aside.

Upper right portion

6 Sew together A22, B19, A23. Sew B20 to the right side of this piecing and set aside.

7 Sew together A24, B21, A25. Sew B22 to the right side, and add A26 to the bottom. Sew to the right side of B20 (the unit that was set aside in Step 1). Set aside again.

8 Sew B23 to A28. Add A27 to the top of this piecing. Sew A29 to B24, and sew to the bottom of the piecing. Sew to the right side of the unit set aside in Step 2. Set aside again.

9 Sew A31 to B25. Add A30 to the left side and A32 to the right. Sew this piecing to the right side of the piecing you set aside in Step 3. Set aside again.

10 Working left to right, assemble A33, B26, A34, B27, A35. Sew B28 to the bottom of this piecing.

11 Finish the upper right portion by sewing this piecing to the top of the piecing you set aside in Step 4.

Lower left portion

12 Sew B14 to A17. Add A16 to the left side and A18 to the right. Working top to bottom, assemble this piecing with B15 and A19. Set aside.

13 Assemble A20, B17, A21. Sew B16 to the left side of this piecing and B18 to the right.

14 Finish the lower left portion by sewing this piecing to the right side of the piecing you set aside in Step 1.

Lower right portion

15 Sew B29 to A37. Add A36 to the left side and A38 to the right. Working top to bottom, assemble this piecing with B30 and A39.

16 Finish the lower right portion by working left to right and assembling this piecing with A40, B31, A41, B32, A42.

Assemble the top

Note: As you work your way through the next steps, be sure to line up all of the various stripes so that the design lines up. Pin as needed to help with this.

17 Sew the 2 upper portions, and join the 2 lower portions.

18 Sew the top and bottom to B13.

Finishing

19 To finish your place mat, layer with your batting and quilt back. Baste using your method of choice. (I like to pin baste.)

20 Quilt as desired. I quilted my place mats with a very simple straight-line pattern to enhance the pieced pattern. I echo-quilted in the white fabric, tracing around all of the black stripes.

21 For the binding, cut 2 strips 2½" (6.5 cm) × width of fabric and piece them together with a diagonal seam. Attach the binding.

Visit **ALISSA HAIGHT CARLTON'S** website at handmadebyalissa.com.

Patchwork Cube Slipcover

by Kevin Kosbab

Why limit yourself to one fabric when there are so many to choose from? Liven up a simple cube-shaped footstool with a mod patchwork slipcover of graphic prints. It's so easy to make you could stitch one for every room.

Materials

— 2 yd (1.8 m) total of assorted home decorator fabrics (see Notes and Steps 1–3)

— Cube-shaped ottoman (shown: 15" × 15" × 15" [38 × 38 × 38 cm] cube; follow Steps 1–3 to adapt the pattern for other cube sizes)

— Heavy-duty sewing thread such as Coats & Clark Dual Duty XP Heavy

— Serger or pinking shears (optional; see Notes)

— Curved upholstery needle (optional)

Finished Size
Varies with ottoman size

notes

* All seam allowances are ½" (1.3 cm) unless otherwise noted.
* For explanations of terms and techniques, see Sewing Basics.
* The sample shown includes twelve different prints; scraps from previous projects work well. The yardage estimate is conservative; the more fabric you have, the more room you'll have for picking out the best motifs. The slipcover could also look stunning in a more subdued palette of differing textures, instead of prints—try finding an out-of-date decorator's swatch book to get just the right amount of many different fabrics economically.
* Zigzag, pink, overcast, or serge all raw edges.
* Press all seams open unless otherwise noted.
* The instructions are for covering a cube, with sides the same dimensions as the top. Adjust the measurements if your ottoman is not a true cube, i.e., if the sides are rectangles rather than squares.

Determine the Measurements

1 Measure each side of your ottoman. To allow ease and make the numbers easier to work with, round up: the sides of this ottoman were approximately 14¾" (37.5 cm) but the measurements were based on a 15" (38 cm) side. This is the minimum amount of ease for a workable slipcover.

2 Divide the side measurements by three to determine the finished size of the patchwork squares, then add ½" (1.3 cm) to each side for seam allowances. For example: 15" (38 cm) side measurement divided by three yields finished squares 5" × 5" (12.5 × 12.5 cm). Adding the ½" (1.3 cm) seam allowances brings the size of the cut squares to 6" × 6" (15 × 15 cm).

3 Add another ½" (1.3 cm) along the bottom side of the lowest row of patches to accommodate a double-fold hem. In the sample, the bottom-row patches were cut to 6" × 6½" (15 × 16.5 cm), including seam and hem allowances.

Cut the Fabric

4 Cut 33 patchwork squares from the assorted fabrics at the dimensions you determined in Step 2 (including seam allowances). If using large-scale prints, choose a different part of the print for each square, keeping in mind that the ½" (1.3 cm) seam allowance on each edge will be hidden. Some of the sample fabrics had birds that fit nicely into the squares; others featured abstract shapes in appealing compositions.

5 Cut 12 bottom-row patches from the assorted fabrics at the dimensions you determined in Step 3. If your prints are directional, note that the shorter edges will be the top and bottom of the finished patch, and plan accordingly when you cut. Also remember that a total of 1" (2.5 cm) of the patch's lower edge will be hidden in the hem.

Piece the Side Panels

6 On a flat surface, arrange your patches into four panels of nine patches each, three patches across and three patches down, using the larger patches in the lowest row of each group. The remaining nine squares will form the top of the slipcover; mark this panel so you can easily differentiate it from the side panels. Rearrange the fabrics until you have a balanced layout, keeping in mind that fabrics from different panels will meet at the seams between the panels.

7 Working on one panel at a time to avoid confusion and sewing with right sides together, assemble the patches into three rows of three patches. Press the seams open.

8 Pin one row to each long side of the middle row, right sides together, aligning the seams between patches (figure 1). Sew and press.

9 Repeat Steps 7–8 to assemble each remaining panel of nine patches. Place the panels against the corresponding sides of the ottoman to double-check the measurements—the panels should be at least 1¼" (3.2 cm) wider than the ottoman and 1¾" (4.5 cm) longer than the ottoman side, including seam and hem allowances.

Assemble the Slipcover

10 Pin two adjacent side panels with right sides together and patch seams aligned. Sew the panels together along one side, beginning ½" (1.3 cm) below the top edge and back-tacking to secure the seam (figure 2). Sew the other two side panels to the first unit in the same way, completing a row of four panels.

11 Join the first and fourth side panels to make a tube, again leaving ½" (1.3 cm) open at the top of the seam. Without turning the tube right-side out, carefully pull it down around the ottoman to test the fit. If an adjustment is necessary, make the seams between panels slightly wider or narrower, distributing the change among all four seams.

12 Pin the top panel into the top of the tube, right sides together, aligning the top panel's corners with the seams between side panels. Work with the side panels on top, and allow the ½" (1.3 cm) left unsewn at the top of each seam to open up at the corners (figure 3). Sew the side panels to the top panel, pivoting around the corners with the needle down.

13 Trim the top corners to reduce bulk, turn the slipcover right-side out, and press.

Finish the Slipcover

14 Slide the slipcover onto the ottoman. The cover should be longer than the ottoman; mark where the fabric reaches the bottom of the ottoman with pins. Remove the slipcover. If the pins are less than 1" (2.5 cm) from the raw edge, adjust the hem measurements accordingly in Step 15. If the pins are more than 1" (2.5 cm) from the raw edge, trim the excess fabric from the lowest row of patches.

15 Fold ½" (1.3 cm) to the wrong side along the bottom of the slipcover and press. Fold an additional ½" (1.3 cm) to the wrong side and press again. Topstitch the hem closed near the inner fold.

16 Slide the finished slipcover onto the ottoman. If necessary, use heavy-duty thread and a curved upholstery needle to tack the cover to the ottoman, invisibly sewing through the hem allowance and the ottoman fabric.

KEVIN KOSBAB regularly designs modern quilts and sewing projects for *Stitch* and other magazines. Find his Feed Dog Designs patterns in stores and on the Web at feeddog.net.

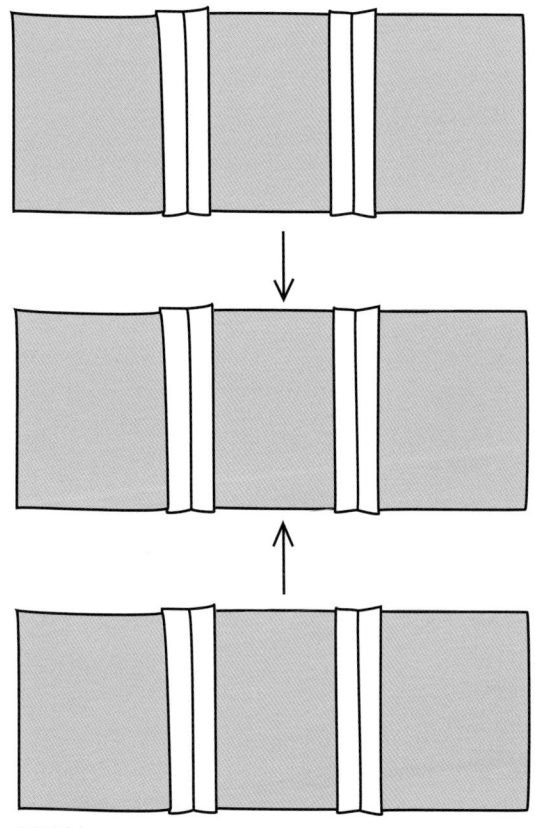

FIGURE 1

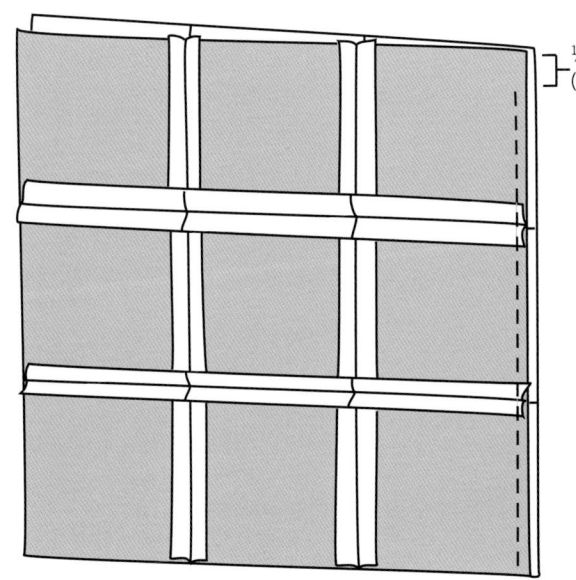

FIGURE 2

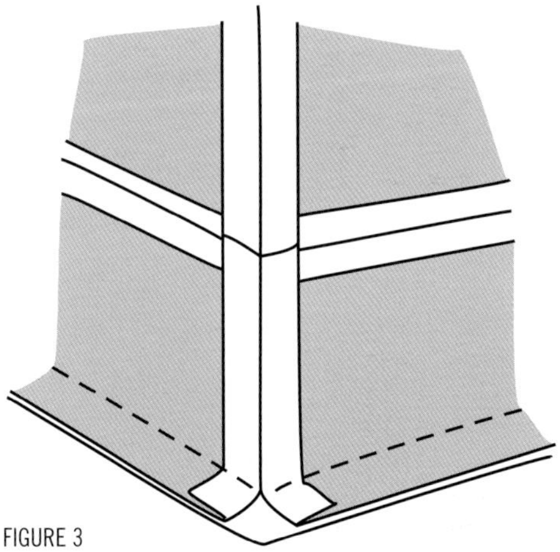

FIGURE 3

PATCHWORK CUBE SLIPCOVER 13

Materials

For the large drawstring bag:
—Bag exterior fabric and lining fabric, one 16" × 8½" (40.5 × 21.5 cm) strip from each

—Drawstring fabric, one 28" × 1" (71 × 2.5 cm) strip

—Safety pin

For the zippered bag:
—Top bag fabric, two 5½" × 9½" (14 × 24 cm) pieces

—Bottom bag fabric, one 6" × 9½" (15 × 24 cm) strip

—Lining fabric, 14" × 9½" (35.5 × 24 cm) piece

—One 9" (23 cm) red zipper

For both bags:
—Thread, in both matching and contrasting colors

—Sewing machine

—Iron and ironing board

Optional
—Materials for decorating the bag fabric (fabric paint, stamps, etc.)

note

✱ Use a ½" (1.3 cm) seam allowance throughout. Press the seams open.

Large Drawstring Bag

My large drawstring bag finishes approximately 7½" wide by 6½" tall (19 × 16.5 cm). I designed it to hold my digital camera components: the USB cable and the charger. Feel free to adjust the cutting sizes to fit your needs, as I did when making my yellow cell phone drawstring bag.

1 Decorate the exterior of the fabric to show what the bag contains. For example, on the outside of my yellow cell phone bag, I simply free-motion satin-stitched numbers in a grid to look like the dial pad on a touch-tone phone. You can use any number of materials and/or techniques to add identifying marks to your fabric, including fabric paint, appliqué, text transfers with gel medium, free-motion quilting, fusible collage, rubber stamps, paint sticks, etc. Be creative and have fun with it.

2 Take the exterior bag fabric and press ¼" (6 mm) to the wrong side along the top edge (one of the 16"

Cable Clutter
CLEANUP BAGS
by Kathy York

These easy-to-make bags are a perfect gift—they'll help the recipient stay organized when at home or while traveling. No longer will you or your loved one search through a drawer of tangled black cables, wondering which is the right one and how to untangle it! These time-saving bags can be used for camera USB cables, camera recharging cables, cell phone chargers, iPod rechargers, etc. The bag size can be easily adjusted to fit your specific needs, and each one can be decorated so it is immediately recognizable. If the inside of your suitcase is black, use a contrasting color to make the bag easy to find. Once you are finished making a few for your friends or family, indulge and make a few for yourself too!

[40.5 cm] long sides), then another ¾" (2 cm), and then iron the folds. Unfold the pressed edges.

3 To sew the side seam, fold the strip in half crosswise with right sides together, sew the top 1" (2.5 cm) of the side seam, and stop, making sure to lock your thread in place. Leave a ¾" (2 cm) gap (this will be the hole for the drawstring later) and begin sewing the rest of the side seam. Continue sewing the side, turn the corner, and stitch the bottom seam.

4 To make the box shape at the bottom of the bag, fold one corner crossways (keeping the bag inside out) so that the side seam lines up with the bottom seam. Pin in place. The side should come out into the point of a triangle. Sew a 2" (5 cm) seam perpendicular to the side and bottom seam, about 1" (2.5 cm) from where the tip makes a point. Repeat for the other side. Trim off the tips of the triangle corners with scissors.

5 Repeat Steps 2–4 with the lining fabric. When completing Step 2, press the top edge in the opposite direction, toward the right side of the fabric.

6 With the bag right-side out, and the lining inside out, place the lining inside the bag. Line up the drawstring gaps in the side seams. Fold down the top edges along the previously pressed folds, folding toward the inside of the bag to create a casing for the drawstring. The edges should be folded ¼" (6 mm) first, and then ¾" (2 cm) to make a finished hem for the casing.

7 From the inside, sew very close to the hem fold of the casing all the way around the bag. The opening for the drawstring should be on the outside of the bag.

8 To create the drawstring, fold the 28" (71 cm) strip of fabric lengthwise into thirds. This will leave a long raw edge on top of a folded edge. Sew an overcast stitch along the length of the strip, leaving the ends open. Attach a safety pin to one end of the drawstring and thread it through the casing. Pull the drawstring until both ends are an even length and then tie small knots in the ends.

9 Locate the point along the drawstring casing that is directly opposite the hole, and staystitch a perpendicular line from the top of the bag to the hem of the drawstring casing. This staystitch should go through the drawstring to keep it from being accidentally pulled through the casing.

Zippered Bag

10 Decorate the exterior fabric to give an indication of the bag contents. For my zippered bag, I kept it simple and just free-motion satin-stitched the words "eye one" on the bottom section. (This bag can hold a one-eye monitor calibration tool; the finished bag measures about 8¼" wide by 5½" tall [21 × 14 cm].)

11 Layer the top bag fabric rectangles with right sides together and machine baste along the top (long) edges with a 1" (2.5 cm) seam allowance. Open the fabrics and press the seam open.

12 Place the zipper right-side down on the wrong side of this unit, centering the teeth directly along the center of the seam; pin it in place. Stitch the zipper to the fabric, sewing along both sides of the zipper. Rip out the basting thread.

13 With right sides together, sew the bottom section of the bag to the top section, first one side and then the other, using ½" (1.3 cm) seam allowances throughout. Press the seam allowances toward the top of the bag.

14 Partially unzip the zipper, line up the side seams, and stitch them. On one side seam, the seam should go through the tabs of the top of the zipper. On the other side seam, fold the excess tail of the zipper toward the center of the bag (still parallel with the zipper). You may need to use the zipper foot to stitch this part of the side seam.

15 To make the box shape at the bottom of the bag, fold one of the corners crossways, so that the side seam lines up with the bottom seam. Pin in place. The seam should come out into the point of a triangle. Sew a 2" (5 cm) seam perpendicular to the side seam, about 1" (2.5 cm) from where the tip makes a point. Repeat for the other side. Trim off the tips of the triangle corners with scissors.

16 Completely unzip the bag and turn it right-side out through the open zipper.

17 Sew the lining by folding the 14" (35.5 cm) side in half and stitching the side seams with a ½" (1.3 cm) seam allowance. Repeat Step 6 for the lining.

18 Place the lining (still wrong-side out) inside the bag and fold the upper raw edge toward the wrong side so the lining fits along the long edges of the zipper tape. Pull the lining back out and press this fold with an iron. It should have a turned-down edge of about ½"–¾" (1.3–2 cm) depending on the fit.

19 Place the lining back inside the bag and handstitch it in place along the zipper tape.

Learn more about **KATHY YORK** at aquamoonartquilts.blogspot.com.

Color Swatch Wall Hanging

by Sheryl Schleicher

Picking out paint chips at the local home improvement store was the inspiration for this quilt. The rows and rows of color on white card stock made me think of quilts. The featured fabrics are from Moda's Grunge collection by Basic Grey.

Materials
For 1 table runner or wall hanging

— Assorted solid fabrics, 30–40 squares or rectangles 2"–2½" × 2"–2½" (5–6.5 × 5–6.5 cm) (Varying the size of the colored fabrics adds interest and creates a more contemporary looking quilt.)

— Background/binding fabric, 1½ yd (137 cm)

— Backing fabric, 25" × 47" (63.5 × 119.5 cm) piece

— Low-loft batting, ¾ yd (68.5 cm)

Finished Size
19" × 41" (48.5 × 104 cm)

Directions

1. From the background fabric, cut 3 strips 2" (5 cm) × WOF (width of fabric).

2. Align the colored squares and rectangles along the right edge of the 2" (5 cm) strips and sew (**figure 1**). Press the seams toward the colored fabrics.

3. Cut the pieced units apart, not worrying if the background fabric is larger than the colored fabric.

4. Plan your fabric arrangement for each strip. Start with a colored fabric and end with the background fabric. (A 3"–4" [7.5–10 cm] length of background fabric on the end allows you more leeway to stagger the strips when you assemble the quilt top.) Sew the pieces together, alternating colored fabric and background fabric, until you have a strip at least 36" (91.5 cm) long (**figure 2**). Make 3 strips.

5. Trim the strips to 1¼" × 36" (3.2 × 91.5 cm) (**figure 3**).

6. From the background fabric, cut 2 strips 6" × 36" (15 × 91.5 cm), 1 strip 5" × 36" (12.5 × 91.5 cm), and 1 strip 3½" × 36" (9 × 91.5 cm).

7. Arrange the pieced strips and background fabric strips as illustrated (**figure 4**). Sew the vertical rows together and press the seams toward the colored strips (**figure 5**). The extra thickness makes it easier to follow the seams when quilting on the background fabric, and it adds dimension to the pieced strips (this will be more apparent once the background is quilted).

Process photos by Sheryl Schleicher

FIGURE 1

FIGURE 2

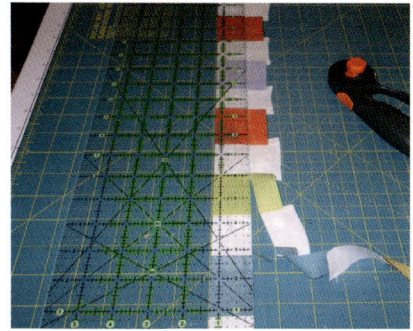
FIGURE 3

8 For the top and bottom, cut 2 strips 3½" × 21¼" (9 × 54 cm). Add these 2 strips and press toward the body of the quilt **(figure 6)**. Layer the backing fabric wrong-side up; add the batting and the quilt top right-side up. Pin or hand baste the layers together.

9 To finish, quilt with straight line quilting, leaving random ¾" (2 cm) gaps as you go. Quilt the seam lines first. Then, using your sewing foot as a guide, sew ¼" (6 mm) away from the first line. Then sew between the 2 lines, splitting the distance as you go. Remember, the best results for straight line quilting come from work that is consistently inconsistent.

10 Bind the quilt.

You can reach **SHERYL SCHLEICHER** by email at sschleic44@gmail.com.

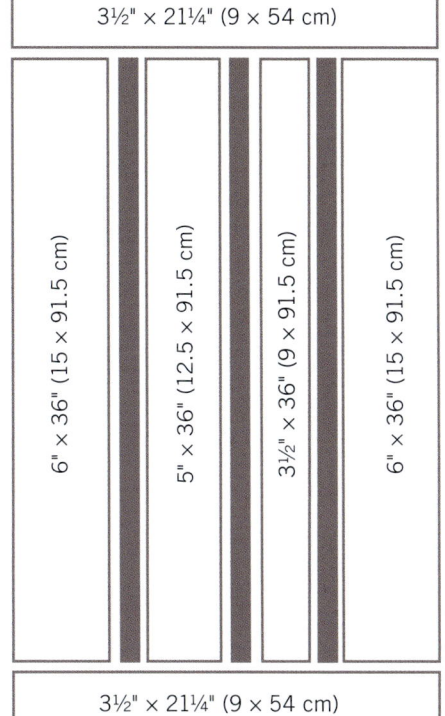
FIGURE 4

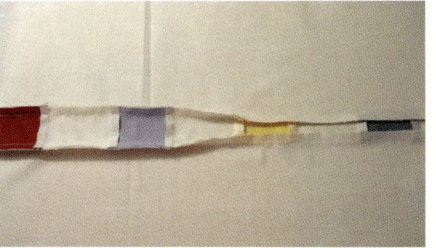
FIGURE 5

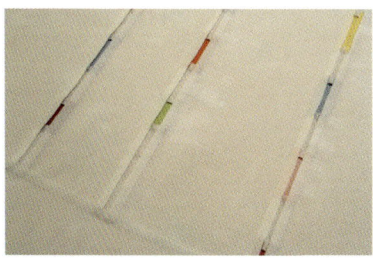
FIGURE 6

COLOR SWATCH WALL HANGING **17**

FIGURE A

How to Hang Small Wall Quilts
USING FRAMING CORNERS
by Sheryl Schleicher

Traditional framing or mounting corners are commonplace for displaying photography, and they can be easily adapted for displaying small wall quilts. Besides being quicker and easier to make than a hanging sleeve, this corner mounting method requires only one hole in the wall.

Materials

—Fabric, 2 squares anywhere from 5" × 5" (12.5 × 12.5 cm) to 9" × 9" (23. × 23 cm), depending on the size of the quilt

—Wooden board (The thickness required depends on the weight of the quilt. For my quilt on page 16 the board is ⅜" [1 cm] thick × 1½" [3.8 cm] wide × 1" [2.5 cm] shorter in length than the quilt width.)

—Handsaw

—Drill with a 1/16" (2 mm) bit

—Pushpin or a nail

FIGURE B

For an Unfinished Quilt

1 After quilting your quilt sandwich, prepare the binding. (I use a 2¼" [5.5 cm] wide strip of fabric, pressed in half.) Machine stitch the binding to the front of the quilt, ¼" (6 mm) from the raw edge.

2 Fold and press the 2 fabric squares in half diagonally, wrong sides together (**figure a**).

3 Do not turn the binding to the back of the quilt yet. Sew the folded fabric corners to the quilt, sewing a scant ⅛" (3 mm) from the edges of the quilt and being careful to stay within the binding seam allowance. There's no need to sew into the corners—the finished binding will secure the fabric.

4 Handsew the binding to the back, being sure to sew all the way through to the backing when stitching along the folded fabric corners.

FIGURE C

5 Cut the wooden hanging bar 1" (2.5 cm) shorter than the finished quilt width (**figure b**). This length allows you to position the quilt as required so it will hang level. Drill a ⅜" (1 cm) hole in the center of the hanging bar. Insert the bar into the corners, and hang on a nail or pushpin. Enjoy!

Note: For a lightweight project, you can use foamcore or thick cardboard for the hanging bar.

Tip

For very small quilts (12" [30.5 cm] or less), you can use leftover binding or strips of fabric instead of framing corners. Fold the fabric lengthwise into a tri-fold and press. Secure the fold with a decorative stitch. Place the fabric strips at a 45-degree angle across the top back corners of the quilt. Secure them with a few stitches or under the binding (**figure c**).

For a Finished Quilt

1 Fold and press the 2 fabric squares in half diagonally, right sides together. Sew the outer edges of the triangles closed. Clip the corners to remove bulk.

2 Cut a slit through 1 layer of fabric on each triangle and turn right-side out. (I precut the slit for turning before I sew.)

3 Press the triangles flat, and pin them to the quilt back (**figure d**).

4 Whipstitch the corners onto the finished binding or just inside the finished binding. The quilt is ready to hang on the wooden framing bar (see Step 5).

FIGURE D

18 MODERN SEWING PROJECTS

Fabric Birds
by Terry Grant

I have been making these birds for a couple of years and find they are fast and fun to construct and a great way to use up small pieces of fabric left over from my quilts and other projects. I especially like using quilting fabrics because these quality cottons are easy to sew and are moldable when stuffed, which helps me to achieve nicely shaped birds, free of wrinkles and puckers.

Choosing the fabrics is the most enjoyable part of this project for me. The bird can be made using just one fabric, or it can be as hodgepodge as you like. I have used commercial fabrics, hand-dyes, my own painted fabrics, and combinations. The wings are a great place to show off an interesting fabric design or combine two fabrics. I am always on the lookout for fabrics that remind me of feathers or have patterns that would work well on a wing. Just centering a striking design motif on each wing can be very effective. Wings also provide an opportunity for embellishment or fancy stitching, which should be done before the bird is assembled.

Materials

— Small pieces (approximately ⅛ yd [11.5 cm]) of cotton quilting fabrics in several colors/patterns that you like together

— Contrasting scrap of cotton fabric for beak, approximately 2" (5 cm) square

— Polyester fiberfill

— Heavyweight fusible interfacing, 6" × 6" (15 × 15 cm) piece (I use Décor-Bond by Pellon.)

— 19-gauge metal wire (I like black, but any color will do.)

— Dark brown floral tape

— Heavy-duty upholstery thread in a compatible color

— Needle for handsewing

— Two glass beads, approximately ⅛" (3 mm) diameter (for eyes)

— Fast-drying fabric glue

— Small wire cutter/pliers

— Stuffing tool or bamboo chopstick

— Bamboo skewer (Blunt the sharp point with an emery board or a piece of sandpaper.)

— Sewing machine and thread to match fabrics

Optional
— Cotton balls

— Clear acrylic medium (I use Golden gloss medium.)

— Paintbrush, 1" (2.5 cm)

Finished Size
About 7" (18 cm) tall

Directions

Gather your fabrics and supplies, and trace and cut out the templates (provided on page 22).

Body

1. Begin by making the leg assembly (see Constructing the Legs & Feet). Set the legs aside.

2. Cut out the fabric and interfacing pieces as indicated on the patterns. Fuse the interfacing pieces to the two outer wing pieces and the beak piece.

3. Stitch the back seam of the two body pieces, right sides facing. Clip the curve and finger-press the seam open.

4. Position the beak piece on the body and pin it in place. (I often glue the beak down instead of pinning. It makes it much easier to keep it in place while you topstitch it.) Use a narrow zigzag stitch along the upper edges to topstitch the beak in place.

5. Press under ¼" (6 mm) along the "opening" seams of both the breast and under-tail pieces.

6. Starting at the point of the beak, carefully pin the breast piece to the body section, right sides together. I find it easiest and most accurate to begin stitching at the point of the beak, and then down one side. I then start again at the point of the beak and stitch the other side.

7. Pin the under-tail to the body, right sides facing, and stitch the sections together.

Constructing the Legs and Feet

1. Cut two pieces of wire 24" (61 cm) long. Using small pliers, bend each piece 13" (33 cm) from one end **(figure 1)**.

2. Using pliers, bend the wire to form a foot, with 4 toes, as follows. The bend you made in the wire will become the first toe. Bend the shorter end of the wire to form the second toe. Bend the longer end of the wire to form the third and fourth toes **(figure 2)**. Crimp each bend with your small pliers to make it as sharp as possible. If the ends of the wire are not exactly even, don't trim them; this is not a problem.

3. Starting with one of the toes, wrap the foot and leg with brown floral tape to enclose the wire **(figure 3)**. The floral tape is somewhat sticky and will stretch and stick to itself so, as you wrap, you can mold the tape to the wire.

4. Bend each leg at a 90-degree angle, 5" (12.5 cm) from the top of the foot. Overlap the ends, as shown, leaving 2¼" (5.5 cm) between the legs. Wrap a small piece of floral tape around the overlapped ends to secure them **(figure 4)**.

5. Bend the legs and feet as shown. The exact angles will be adjusted after the bird is assembled. Bend the ends into semicircles, one in front of the leg assembly and one in back, as shown **(figure 5)**. This will be buried in the stuffing of the bird to give it stability.

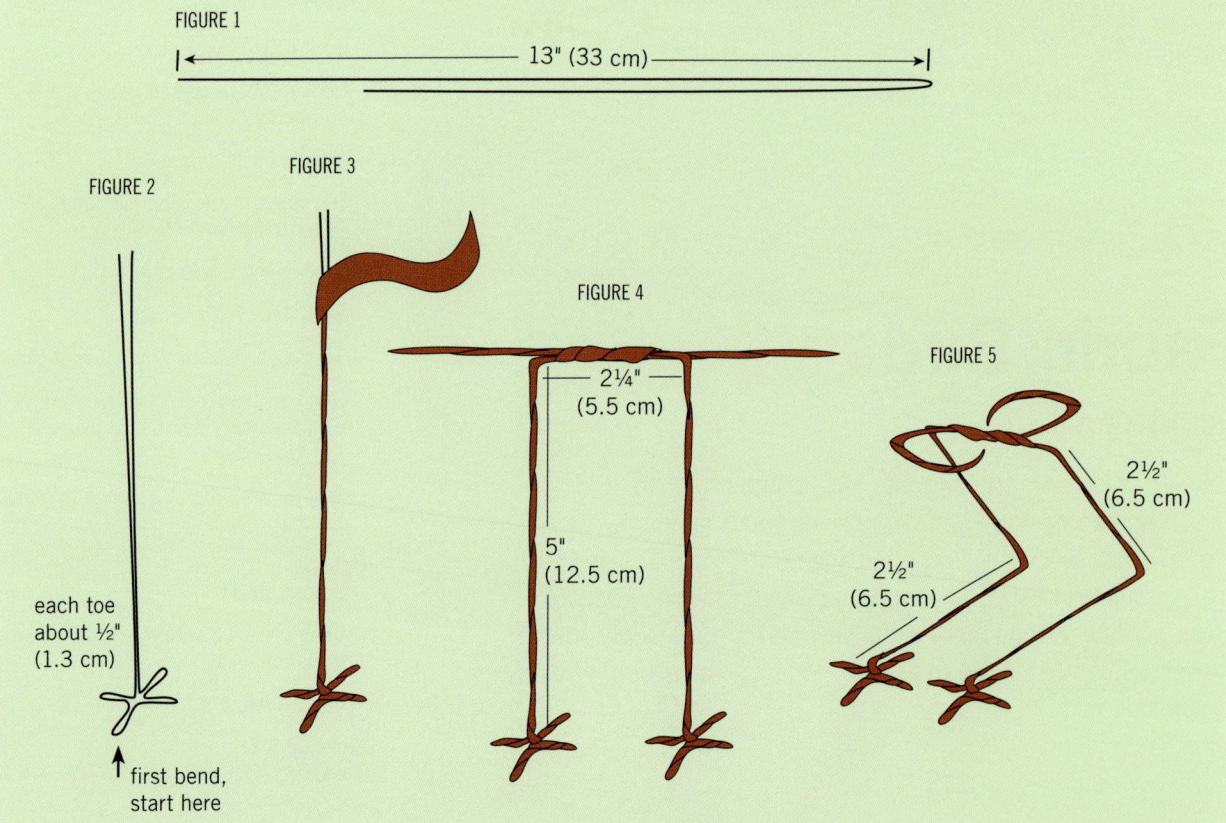

8 Trim the seam around the beak and at the end of the tail to within 1/16" (2 mm) of the stitching.

9 Turn the body right-side out through the opening. Carefully poke the beak out, using the blunt end of the bamboo skewer. If necessary, use the sharper end of the skewer, taking great care to avoid poking through the fabric or popping the seam. Use the skewer to completely turn the tail section right-side out.

10 Stuff the body, starting with the beak and head, and then stuff the tail. Use plenty of stuffing to make the bird very firm; it will probably take more than you think. You may find it helpful to use a stuffing tool or a bamboo chopstick to compress the stuffing into the corners and smaller areas.

> **Tip**
> Polyester fiberfill is very slippery and tends to slide out of very small areas like the beak. I use a bit of cotton (from cosmetic cotton balls) to stuff the beak since it stays in place. Then I continue stuffing the rest of the bird with fiberfill.

11 When the body feels nearly full, insert the leg assembly into the opening. One of the top wire loops should extend into the breast area, and the other into the under-tail area. Be sure the legs are facing the correct direction and that they exit the body at the seam line at each side of the opening. Work a little extra stuffing between the wire loops and inside the fabric to pad them and make them invisible from the outside.

12 Close the opening using heavy-duty thread. A ladder stitch will make a nearly invisible seam.

Ladder stitch

> **Tip**
> If the seams don't look smooth after the bird is stuffed, or if the head needs to be smoothed and rounded a bit, spritz the seams with a little water and carefully run the tip of a hot iron over them.

13 Using the same heavy-duty thread, stitch the beads into place for the eyes. Run the thread through the head to attach a bead to each side. Pull the thread to slightly indent the eyes—not too much, or the bird will look cross-eyed!

Wings

14 Layer the fused outer wing and inner wing together, right sides out.

15 Stitch 1/4" (6 mm) from the edge all the way around the wing.

16 Trim the wing close to the stitching, through all layers. You can leave the wing like this, or enclose the edge with decorative stitching, either by hand or machine. Make the second wing in the same manner.

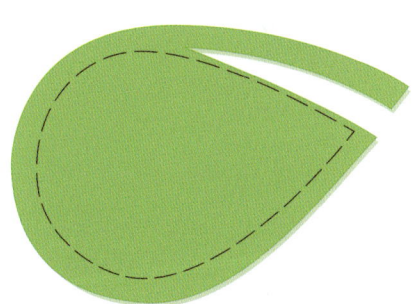

FABRIC BIRDS 21

17 Complete any additional embellishment you want on the wings.

18 Pin the wings to the bird's body, positioning them as you like, and leaving the wing edges loose. Carefully apply a narrow bead of fabric glue around the inside, rounded end of the wing, extending approximately between the widest points of the wing. Hold the wing firmly against the body until the glue sets.

Finishing

19 When the bird is finished and the glue is dry, you may want to coat the bird with a layer of acrylic medium to seal it. (I find they are much easier to keep clean if I do this.) Dilute some clear acrylic medium with a little water and brush it over all the fabric parts of the bird. Be sure to test the medium on a scrap of fabric first. I have found that some brands leave a milky haze on the fabric and dull the color.

20 You will need to adjust the legs to make your bird stand on its own. Bend the toes slightly to give them a more natural appearance. Some birds seem to like to stand up taller with straighter legs; others balance better a little closer to the ground.

21 You will find that every bird you make will look a little different and take on its own individual personality.

TERRY GRANT'S work has been featured in *Quilting Arts Magazine*, the book *Creative Quilting: The Journal Quilt Project,* and other publications. Visit her blog at andsewitgoes.blogspot.com.

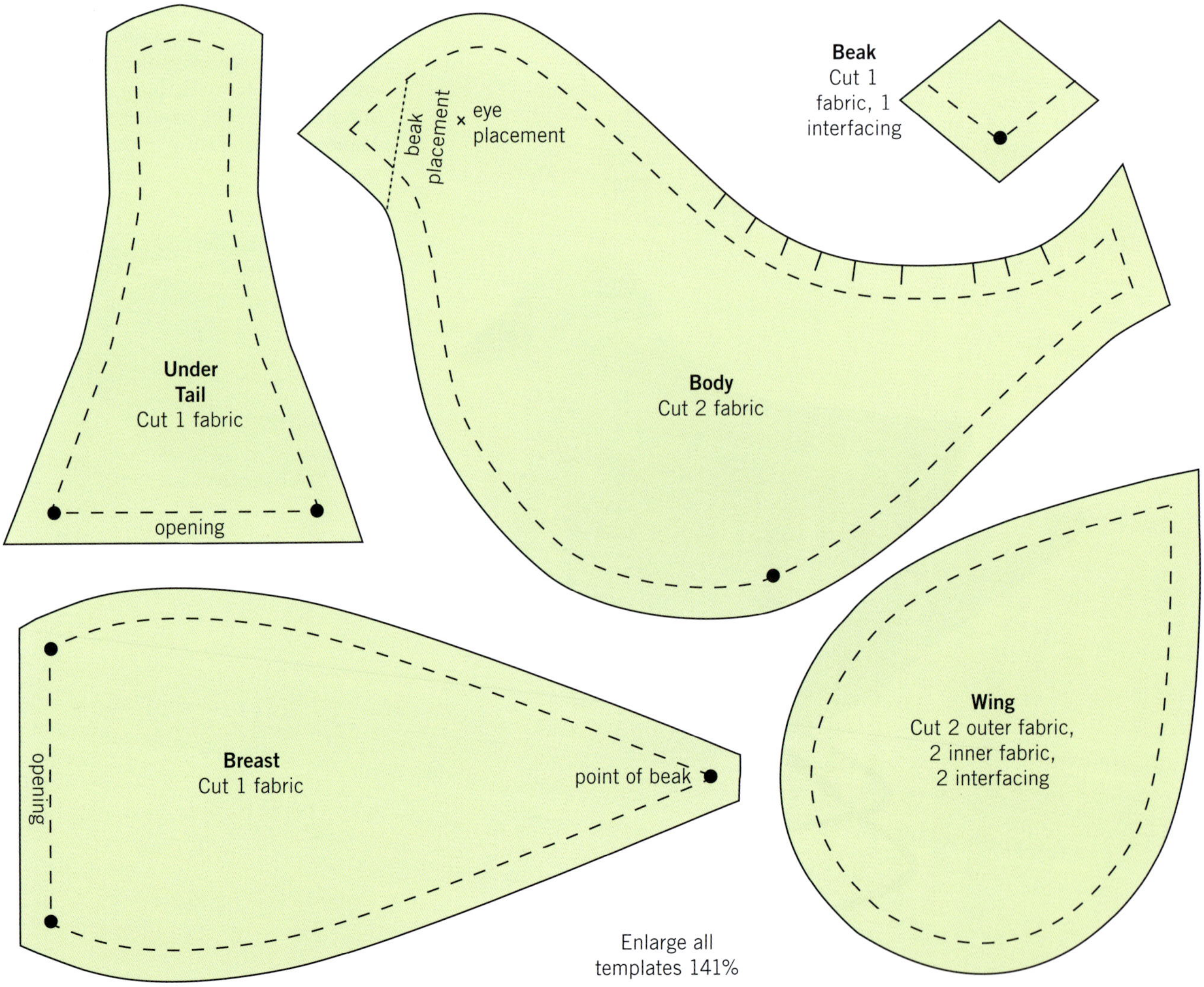

Under Tail Cut 1 fabric
opening

Body Cut 2 fabric
beak placement × eye placement

Beak Cut 1 fabric, 1 interfacing

Breast Cut 1 fabric
opening
point of beak

Wing Cut 2 outer fabric, 2 inner fabric, 2 interfacing

Enlarge all templates 141%

22 MODERN SEWING PROJECTS

The size of this quilt makes it a great throw for the couch, or you could increase (or decrease) the number of blocks to make a bed or crib quilt.

The quilt top is made up of two types of blocks: 12½" (31.5 cm) squares of print fabrics (these can be one fabric cut to 12½" [31.5 cm], or you can choose to sew two fabrics together and then cut the pieced unit to 12½"[31.5 cm]) and the Rubik's block, which consists of a small patchwork square that is sashed with a light-colored solid fabric. The Rubik's blocks are bordered with the same solid fabric. To add interest, I elected to center some of the Rubik's centers and to offset the remaining ones; these instructions will lead you to do likewise.

Materials
— Assorted print fabrics, (18) 12½" (31.5 cm) squares and (153) 2½" (6.5 cm) squares

— Light-colored solid fabric for the Rubik's block sashing, 2 yards

Finished Size
55" × 77" (139.5 × 195.5 cm)

Directions

Cutting the solid fabric
Note: Cut all strips across the full width of the fabric, from selvedge to selvedge.

1 Cut (14) 1" (2.5 cm) strips. Subcut the strips to get a total of (102) 2½" (6.5 cm) lengths, and (34) 7½" (19 cm) lengths.

2 Cut (5) 3¼" (8.5 cm) strips, (2) 4" (10 cm) strips, (2) 2½" (6.5 cm) strips, (2) 4½" (11.5 cm) strips, (2) 2" (5 cm) strips, (2) 5" (12.5 cm) strips, and (2) 1½" (3.8 cm) strips. From each of these strips, cut (2) 7½" (19 cm) lengths and (2) 13" (33 cm) lengths.

The block centers
3 Select (9) 2½" (6.5 cm) square blocks and arrange them on your work surface in 3 rows, 3 blocks per row. Position a 1" × 2½" (2.5 × 6.5 cm) strip of solid fabric between each square.

4 Sew each row as follows: small block, solid strip, small block, solid strip, small block. Iron flat,

Rubik's Crush
by Ashley Newcomb

This is a fun quilt to showcase a favorite fabric collection, especially one with large-scale prints, such as Anna Maria Horner's Innocent Crush collection for FreeSpirit. This quick quilt contains plenty of interest, pairing large print squares with more intricate pieced blocks, which I think resemble a Rubik's Cube.

pressing all seams open. Repeat for each row.

5 Sew the 3 rows together alternately with (3) 1" × 7½" (2.5 × 19 cm) solid strips. Press the seams open. The pieced square should measure 7½" × 7½" (19 × 19 cm; raw edge to raw edge). Make a total of 17 block centers.

Sashing

Note: Once the outer strips are added to each block center, the block will measure 13" × 13" (33 × 33 cm), and it will be necessary to trim each block to 12½" (31.5 cm) square.

Centered block

6 Sew (1) 3¼" × 7½" (8.5 × 19 cm) solid strip to the top of a Rubik's block center, and sew (1) 3¼" × 7½" (8.5 × 19 cm) solid strip to the bottom. Press the seams open.

7 Sew a 3¼" × 13" (8.5 × 33 cm) solid strip to each side of the block. Press the seams open. Trim the block to 12½" × 12½" (31.5 × 31.5 cm). Make a total of 5 blocks.

Off-center block #1

8 Sew (1) 2½" × 7½" (6.5 × 19 cm) solid strip to the top of a Rubik's block center, and sew (1) 4" × 7½" (10 × 19 cm) solid strip to the bottom. Press the seams open.

9 Sew (1) 2½" × 13" (6.5 × 33 cm) solid strip to 1 side, and sew (1) 4" × 13" (10 × 33 cm) solid strip to the opposite side of the block. Press the seams open, and trim the block. Make 4 blocks.

Off-center block #2

10 Sew (1) 2" × 7½" (5 × 19 cm) solid strip to the top of a Rubik's block center, and sew (1) 4½" × 7½" (11.5 × 19 cm) solid strip to the bottom. Press the seams open.

11 Sew (1) 2" × 13" (5 × 33 cm) solid strip to 1 side, and sew (1) 4½" × 13" (11.5 × 33 cm) solid strip to the opposite side of the block. Press the seams open, and trim the block to size. Make 4 blocks.

Off-center block #3

12 Sew (1) 1½" × 7½" (3.8 × 19 cm) solid strip to the top of a Rubik's block center, and sew (1) 5" × 7½" (12.5 × 19 cm) solid strip to the bottom. Press the seams open.

13 Sew (1) 1½" × 13" (3.8 × 33 cm) solid strip to 1 side of the block, and sew (1) 5" × 13" (12.5 × 33 cm) solid strip to the opposite side. Press the seams open. Trim the block to size. Make 4 blocks.

The Quilt Top

Note: There are seven rows of 5 squares each (alternating print squares with pieced Rubik's blocks).

14 For the first row, alternate 1 print 12½" (31.5 cm) square with 1 Rubik's block, starting with the print square. Arrange your blocks as desired, balancing out the color placement. Sew the blocks together and press the seams open.

15 Sew the second row, starting with a Rubik's block and alternating the Rubik's blocks with the print 12½" (31.5 cm) squares. Press the seams open.

16 Continue this pattern to make all 7 rows.

17 Sew the rows together, pressing the seams open.

Finishing

18 Layer the backing, batting, and top. Baste as desired.

19 Free-motion quilt as desired.

20 Square up the quilt and trim as needed. Attach the binding, following your preferred binding method.

Visit **ASHLEY NEWCOMB** online at filminthefridge.com.

Reusable Produce Bags

by Lisa Chin

A few years ago I started using reusable grocery bags and now I love being plastic bag free. However, there was always another dilemma when I visited the grocery store—should I have fruits and vegetables rolling willy-nilly about the cart, or use a plastic bag? While reading Angelina Hook's blog (strawberrystitches.blogspot.com), I was inspired by her sewn produce bags. I decided to modify the pattern to suit my needs. I discovered that grosgrain ribbon (used for the drawstring) washes best; a mini-barrel cord stop is lightweight, making it easy to tie the bag; and using mosquito netting allows the bags to be used to carry bulk items such as rice, beans, and nuts. Smaller and larger bags can be made by adjusting the length of the netting and the width of all fabrics. I have sewn dozens of these reusable produce bags in many sizes, even long bags for baguettes, and my friends just keep requesting more!

Materials

To make (2) 10½" × 16" (26.5 × 40.5 cm) bags

— 2½" (6.5 cm) × WOF (width of fabric) strip of cotton fabric for bag top

— 4" (10 cm) × WOF strip of cotton fabric for bag bottom

— 12" (30.5 cm) × WOF strip of mosquito netting

— 2 yd (183 cm) of ¼" (6 mm) grosgrain ribbon, cut into (2) 1 yd (91.5 cm) lengths

— 2 mini-barrel cord stops

Directions

Cutting

1 Remove the selvedges from your cotton fabric strips, and then cut the strips in half (yielding 4 pieces about 22" [56 cm] long each).

> **Tip**
>
> I use mosquito netting because it is lightweight and softer on fruits and vegetables than tulle or netting. It also washes beautifully and sews easier than other options. Mosquito netting is readily available online and I have also found it at my local fabric store.

2 Matching the selvedges, fold the mesh in half. Cutting from the selvedge, cut the mesh into 2 pieces 12" × 22" (30.5 × 56 cm) or shorter if your fabric strips are shorter than 22" (56 cm); just make sure the mesh and fabric strips are all the same length.

Note: There is no need to remove the selvedges from the mesh. The short piece of mesh leftover at the fold can be used to make smaller bags later.

Sew the bag

3 Take (1) 2½" (6.5 cm) wide fabric strip, (1) 4" (10 cm) wide fabric strip, and (1) piece of mesh. (Set aside the additional fabric strips and mesh. These will be used to make a second bag.) Using a ¼" (6 mm) seam, stitch the 2½" (6.5 cm) strip of cotton fabric to 1 of the long sides of the mesh for the bag top.

4 Stitch the 4" (10 cm) strip of cotton fabric to the other long side of

REUSABLE PRODUCE BAGS **25**

the mesh for the bag bottom. (There is no wrong or right side to the mesh; just make sure that both pieces of cotton fabric are on the same side of the mesh.)

5 Zigzag or serge to finish both seams.

Buttonhole and drawstring

6 Make a ½" (1.3 cm) buttonhole at the center of the top cotton fabric strip. The buttonhole should start 1½" (3.8 cm) down from the raw edge of the strip.

7 Fold 1 length of ribbon in half and slip the folded end through the buttonhole from the wrong side.

8 Slip the fold of the ribbon into the cord stop, pull it through a few inches, and make a slipknot at the fold to prevent the cord stop from coming off.

9 Baste 1 loose end of the ribbon to each end of the top strip (1½" [3.8 cm] down from the top of the strip).

Finish

10 Make a tube on top by folding under ¼" (6 mm) along the long raw edge. Then, fold the top strip in half lengthwise with wrong sides together, making sure to tuck the serged seam inside the tube.

11 Topstitch the tube, making sure not to catch the ribbon in the stitching.

12 Fold the entire piece in half with right sides together.

13 Using a ¼" (6 mm) seam, stitch together the side and bottom of the bag. Finish the edges by serging or zigzag stitching. Turn your bag right-side out and put it to use!

14 To make a second bag, simply repeat the process, or you can try experimenting with fabric and mesh sizes to create a variety of bags for different purposes.

Visit **LISA CHIN** online at somethingcleveraboutnothing.blogspot.com.

Travel Lingerie BAG

by Blair Stocker

Carry along your favorite undergarments in this sweet travel bag featuring charming lace appliqués. One side for clean, one side for dirty, and space for your travel slippers in the middle, all separated and compact!

Materials

- ½ yd (45.5 cm) medium-weight fabric for body (Main; home decorator fabric or soft canvas works well)
- ½ yd (45.5 cm) quilting-weight cotton for lining (Lining; shown: Paris Bebe fabric by Robin Mynatt)
- Scraps of laces and quilting-weight cotton fabrics in various prints for appliqués
- ½ yd (45.5 cm) or 1 package light-weight fusible web
- Washable fabric glue
- Embroidery floss in various colors to complement your appliqués (*shown:* orange, light brown, tan, white, blue, and yellow)
- 10" (25.5 cm) of 1" (2.5 cm) wide sew-in Velcro
- Coordinating sewing thread
- Two 12" (30.5 cm) zippers in colors to match or coordinate with Main fabric
- Disappearing-ink fabric marker
- Dressmaker's carbon paper (optional)
- Tracing wheel, dry ballpoint pen, or knitting needle (optional)
- Embroidery needle
- Handsewing needle
- Zipper foot for sewing machine
- Appliqué templates on page 29

Finished Size
21" × 12" (53.5 × 30.5 cm) unfolded, 10½" × 12" (26.5 × 30.5 cm) folded

notes

* All seam allowances are ½" (1.3 cm) unless otherwise indicated.
* For explanations of terms and techniques, see Sewing Basics.
* Templates provided are full size.
* The lightweight fusible web works well on both lace and fabric. To avoid leaving any adhesive residue on your iron or ironing board, cover the ironing board and the fabric appliqué with parchment paper or nonstick pressing sheets.

Directions

Cut fabric

1 Cut 2 pieces of the Main fabric, each 22" × 13" (56 × 33 cm).

2 Cut 2 pieces of the Lining fabric, each 22" × 13" (56 × 33 cm).

Prepare appliqué and embroidery designs

3 Trace each of the appliqué templates onto the paper side of the fusible web. Roughly cut around each traced shape.

4 Gather the scrap fabrics and laces for the appliqués. Apply the fusible web to the wrong side of the desired fabric or lace following the manufacturer's instructions.

5 Cut each appliqué shape along the traced outline and set aside for Step 9.

6 Fold one Main fabric piece in half widthwise, wrong sides together, and press a crease at the fold. Now lay the piece flat, right-side up, on your work surface.

7 Draw the clothesline for each side of the bag on the Main fabric freehand with a disappearing-ink fabric marker, making a gentle curve across the bag width and referring to the template for guidance; or, as an alternative, lay dressmaker's tracing paper on the Main fabric, position the template on top, and trace the clothesline with a tracing wheel, dry ballpoint pen, or knitting needle tip.

8 Add the words "Wash" and "Wear" in the same manner as the clothesline (refer to the diagram and templates on pages 28 and 29 for placement).

FIGURE 1

Appliqué and embroider

9 Following the layout on the templates and in the diagram, peel the paper off the back of the garment appliqué pieces and fuse them onto the right side of the body fabric, being careful to adhere each garment securely to the fabric. For the gathered skirt on the Wear side, pinch one end of the appliqué fabric before fusing to create gathers. Use a small amount of fabric glue for any edges that don't adhere well. Do this for all the pieces.

10 Using 2 strands of coordinating embroidery thread, sew a running stitch around each garment, 1/16" to 1/8" (2 to 3 mm) inside the raw edge, to further secure them onto the bag and add a decorative element.

11 To stitch the clotheslines, use 3 strands of embroidery floss in a color of your choice (shown: orange). Use a running stitch and follow the lines you've drawn. Remove the markings with water or according to the pen manufacturer's instructions.

12 Backstitch the words "Wash" and "Wear" using 3 strands of embroidery floss in the color of your choice (shown: blue).

Add Velcro and zippers

13 Separate the strip of Velcro. Position one half of the

TRAVEL LINGERIE BAG 27

hook-and-loop fastener on each end of the remaining Main fabric piece (the one without appliqués), centering the strip 2" (5 cm) below each end of the fabric (**figure 1**). Edgestitch around all four sides of each strip.

14 Position the 2 Main fabric panels right sides together, raw edges matched, and using a basting stitch (4.0 mm long), sew a ½" (1.3 cm) seam along one of the 13" (33 cm) sides. Press the seam allowances open.

15 With the joined panels wrong-side up, center the zipper teeth right-side down over the seam. Make sure the stops at each end of the zipper do not fall on the ½" (1.3 cm) seam line where the panels will later be joined at the sides. Hand baste the zipper tape to the seam allowances on each side, through all layers, to hold it in place.

16 With the fabric facing right-side up and using a zipper foot and coordinating thread, stitch the zipper through all layers, ¼" (6 mm) away from the teeth, on each side of the zipper.

17 Using your seam ripper, carefully remove the basting stitches from Step 15. The zipper should open freely.

18 Repeat Steps 14 through 17 on the remaining 13" (33 cm) side with the second zipper.

bag diagram

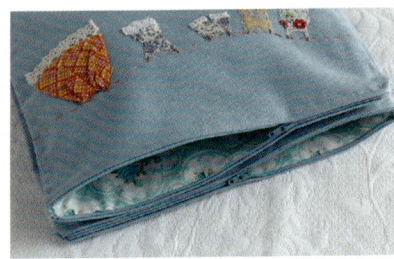

Sew bag and add lining

19 Open each zipper halfway, so the slide lies near the middle of the bag. Place the bag pieces right sides together, raw edges matched (the zippers will now be right sides together as well), and sew the side seams. Make sure the needle doesn't hit the zipper stops as you sew across the zippers. Turn the bag right-side out and press.

20 Following the crease you ironed across the center in Step 6 (fold and press again, if necessary), sew a straight stitch across the bag, through all layers, dividing it in half widthwise. You now have the completed bag shell.

21 Fold ½" (1.3 cm) of each short end of the lining pieces to the wrong side and press. Fold each lining panel in half widthwise right sides together, matching the raw edges. Stitch the sides of each lining, leaving the pressed edges open. With the bag shell right-side out and the lining wrong side out, insert one lining into each side of the bag, gently pushing into place.

22 Slip-stitch the lining's pressed edges to the zipper tape to secure it in place.

See more from **BLAIR STOCKER** on her blog, *wise craft,* at blairpeter.typepad.com.

28 MODERN SEWING PROJECTS

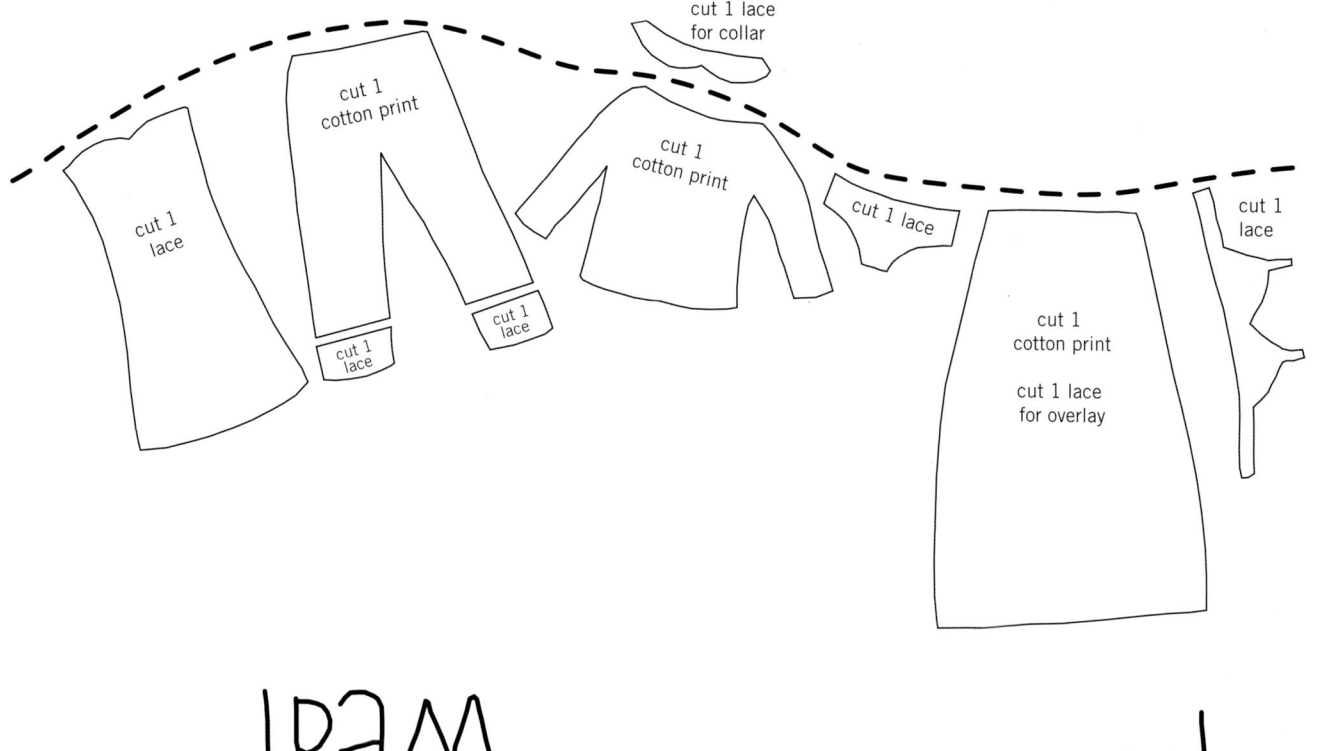

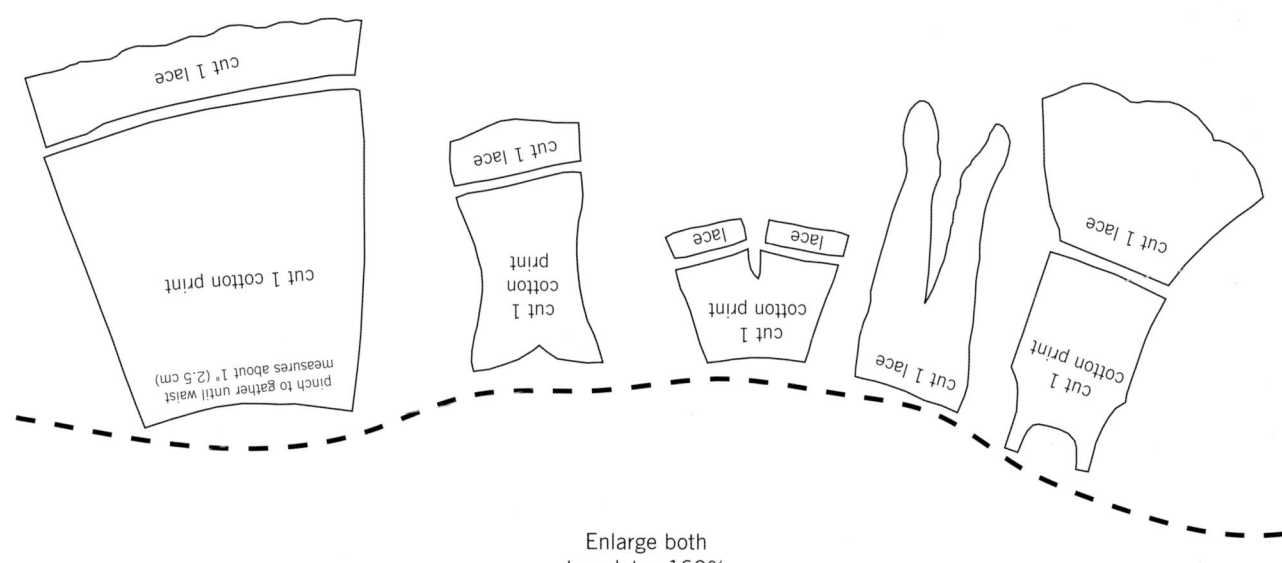

Enlarge both templates 160%

TRAVEL LINGERIE BAG

Alphabet Baby Quilt
by Erin Gilday

This easy-to-make retro alphabet quilt is a breeze for the first-time quilter. The colorful, oversized felt appliqué letters and fun-to-follow squares are sure to keep baby enthralled, and the soft flannel quilt backing is perfect for snuggly naptime.

Materials
— 1 sheet light blue felt (a)
— 1 sheet purple felt (b)
— 1 sheet orange felt (c)
— 2 sheets yellow felt (d)
— 2 sheets black felt (e)
— 3 sheets dark green felt (f)
— 3 sheets fuchsia felt (g)
— 4 sheets cerulean blue felt (h)
— ¼ yd (23 cm) pink felt (i)
— ¼ yd (23 cm) lime green felt (j)
— ½ yd (45.5 cm) white felt (k)
— ½ yd (45.5 cm) gray felt (l)
— 1⅝ yd (1.5 m) 45" (114.5 cm) wide black and white mini check for quilt top (m)
— 1⅝ yd (1.5 m) 45" (114.5 cm) wide gray flannel for quilt back (n)
— Fusible web
— Coordinating sewing thread
— 1 crib-size (45" × 60" [114.5 cm × 152.5 cm]) batting
— 190" (483 cm) of ⅞" (2.2 cm) wide double-fold bias quilt binding
— Fabric marking pen or tailor's chalk
— Bent-arm quilting safety pins
— Letter templates on pages 33–34

Finished Size
52½" × 37½" (133.5 × 95 cm).

notes
* For explanations of terms and techniques, see Sewing Basics.
* Most of the appliqués can be cut from 9" × 12" (23 × 30.5 cm) sheets of felt, but you'll need several colors by the yard to accommodate a few oversized blocks. Felt yardages are given for 72" (183 cm) wide felt. Use the colors listed below or desired colors. Assign each fabric a letter a–n as indicated, especially if using different colors than those listed.

Piecing the Quilt Top

1 Refer to the Cutting Table on page 31. Transfer the letter templates to the felt. Use the templates as patterns, pin them to the felt, and cut around the pattern shapes or trace around the templates with a fabric marking pen or chalk before cutting. Flip the templates over and trace on the felt wrong side, if desired, to be sure no marks will be visible in the finished quilt. Cut out each letter and the pieces that are appliquéd on top of some letters.

2 Using a zigzag stitch (2.5–3.0 mm wide × 1.4–1.6 mm long) and matching thread, appliqué the letters to felt squares, using the photo and the Cutting Table at right as guides to sizes and colors. If desired, use a larger stitch for the large letters, or experiment with other machine stitches. The felt won't ravel, so it's not necessary to cover the appliqué edges with stitches. Don't worry about stabilizing—the felt should stay in place all by itself. Position and appliqué the holes in the A, O, etc., after the main portion of the letter is stitched to the felt square. When the appliqué is complete, back each square with fusible web.

3 Cut a 53" × 38" (134.5 × 96.5 cm) quilt top from the mini check fabric and refer to the diagram for letter placement, arranging the blocks within a 49" × 34" (124.5 × 86.5 cm) area at the center of the fabric (see the photo above for placement, if desired) and leaving a 2" (5 cm) margin between the extreme perimeter of the block of squares and the edge of the quilt top. When you're satisfied with the placement, fuse each letter block firmly to the quilt top according to the fusible web manufacturer's instructions. Allow the web to cool before sewing through it; otherwise, it will gum up your needle.

4 Appliqué each block to the quilt top with coordinating thread, using a zigzag stitch as before.

Quilting the Quilt

5 Cut a 56" × 41" (142 × 104 cm) quilt back from the flannel. Cut a piece of batting to the same size.

6 Make a quilt sandwich with the quilt back on the bottom (right-side down), batting in the middle, and quilt top on top (right-side up). Smooth the sandwich so that there are no wrinkles or puckers at any point in the quilt. The quilt top is slightly smaller than the backing and batting to allow for shrinkage during quilting. Pin all 3 layers together using quilting safety pins. Distribute pins generously, about one pin every 4"–6" (10–15 cm).

7 Using a straight stitch, quilt through all 3 layers around each block, about ½" (1.3 cm) outside the edge of the block. Some variation in the quilting stitch placement adds to the quilt's free-form style. Roll the excess quilt up to fit under the arm of your sewing machine and remove pins as you go.

Finishing the Edges

8 When you've quilted around each letter block, trim the batting and backing to match the quilt top edges. The finished measurements of the quilt should be about 52½" × 37½" (133.5 × 95 cm). Square up the edges if necessary. Baste the layers together along the perimeter of the quilt, ¼" (6 mm) away from the edge.

Cutting Table

Felt Color	Letters to Cut	Backgrounds to Cut (corresponding letter appliqué indicated)
Light blue (a)	X	C: 4⅝" × 3¾" (11.7 × 9.5 cm) R: 3⅜" × 5" (8.6 × 12.5 cm)
Purple (b)	F O interior detail U	
Orange (c)	L "AND" interior details	I: 4½" × 3" (11.5 × 7.5 cm) P: 3¼" × 4⅝" (8.5 × 11.7 cm)
Yellow (d)		U: 5¾" × 5½" (14.5 × 14 cm) F: 6" × 8" (15 × 20.5 cm)
Black (e)	H V	Z: Smaller star
Dark green (f)	A interior detail D J P Q interior detail R T W	
Fuchsia (g)	K S Y	B: 5⅜" × 4" (13.7 × 10 cm) H: 4¾" × 4¾" (12 × 12 cm) X: 4¼" × 3½" (11 × 9 cm)
Cerulean blue (h)	C E I N "AND"	K: 5¼" × 11¾" (13.5 × 30 cm)
Pink yardage (i)	O	E: 8¼" × 8¼" (21 × 21 cm) J: 4½" × 4¼" (11.5 × 11 cm) ST: 11" × 8¾" (28 × 22 cm) AND: 5½" × 10" (14 × 25.5 cm)
Lime green yardage (j)	A Q R interior detail Z	L: 6" × 5½" (15 × 14 cm) J: 4½" × 4¼" (11.5 × 11 cm)
White yardage (k)	B G M P interior detail	D: 3⅝" × 4" (9.2 × 10 cm) Q: 4⅛" × 5⅛" (10.5 × 13 cm) Z: Larger star
Gray yardage (l)		A: 14½" × 10¾" (37 × 27.5 cm) G: 15¼" × 7½" (38.5 × 19 cm) MNO: 11¼" × 16" (28.5 × 40.5 cm) Y: 5⅝" × 10" (14.3 × 25.5 cm) V: 5⅞" × 5¾" (14.9 × 14.5 cm)

9 Following the instructions under Binding with Mitered Corners, option A, on page 32, place the binding with the back of the quilt facing up. Where instructed to slip-stitch the binding, use the following instructions instead. Using a wide zigzag stitch, stitch along the quilt binding edge, positioning the stitch so the right swing of the zigzag catches the binding and the left swing enters the quilt just beyond the binding's folded edge. Sew with the top of the quilt facing up. Press the quilt flat. Whipstitch the mitered corners closed by hand.

ERIN GILDAY offers free sewing tutorials at patchworkunderground.com.

Enlarge all templates 400%

ALPHABET BABY QUILT 33

Enlarge all templates 400%

Yoga Mat CARRIER
by Vivika Hansen DeNegre

Arrive at your next yoga class with your mat rolled in a stylish cover. This yoga mat carrier features an optional zippered interior pocket and an adjustable shoulder strap, leaving your hands free for the rest of your gear. It is edged in Ultrasuede for durability and comfort, and is easy to make.

Materials
— 4–5 coordinating fabrics cut into strips that measure 1"–3" (2.5–7.5 cm) wide by 20" (51 cm) long (Depending on the strip width, you will need approximately 14 strips.)

— Fabric scraps for covered buttons

— Fabric for shoulder strap: 1 strip 2½" × 62" (6.5 × 157.5 cm; can be pieced)

— Backing fabric: 19" × 14" (48.5 × 35.5 cm)

— Batting: 19" × 14" (48.5 × 35.5 cm)

— Ultrasuede cut into:
(2) 2" × 18½" (5 × 47 cm) strips (top and bottom borders)
(2) 1½" × 13½" (3.8 × 34.5 cm) strips (side borders)
(2) 1" × 4" (2.5 × 10 cm) strips (to hold metal loops)

— 2 rectangular metal strap holders (to fit 1" [2.5 cm] wide fabric loops)

— Slide buckle (for adjustable strap)

— (3) 1" (2.5 cm) buttons

— (3) large ponytail elastics

Optional
— 7" (18 cm) zipper

— Ultrasuede cut into (1) 2½" × 6½" (6.5 × 16.5 cm) rectangle and (1) 11½" × 6½" (29 × 16.5 cm) rectangle for pocket

— ½" × 62" (1.3 × 157.5 cm) strip of Ultrasuede for shoulder strap decoration (can be pieced)

— Covered button kit to make (3) 1" (2.5 cm) buttons

Finished Size
13½" × 18½" (34.5 × 47 cm) with adjustable strap

Directions

1 Sew the strips of coordinating fabrics together to make a pleasing striped pattern for the top of the carrier. Press all of the seams in one direction, and trim the piece to 19" × 14" (48.5 × 35.5 cm).

2 Layer the pieced top with the batting and backing, and quilt it with close, undulating lines. Trim the edges of the quilted piece to 18½" × 13½" (47 × 34.5 cm).

YOGA MAT CARRIER **35**

3 Sew a 2" × 18½" (5 × 47 cm) strip of Ultrasuede to the back side of 1 long edge of the piece, right sides together. Fold the Ultrasuede over the edge to the front and topstitch it in place.

4 Optional pocket: Sew the zipper between the 11½" × 6½" (29 × 16.5 cm) strip of Ultrasuede on 1 side, and a 2½" × 6½" (6.5 × 16.5 cm) rectangle of Ultrasuede on the other side. Fold the rectangle in half with right sides together (the fold should be parallel to the zipper); stitch the 2 sides (perpendicular to the zipper). Turn the pocket right-side out. Position it faceup on the back of the carrier on the side opposite the side you just finished, and pin it in place.

5 Repeat Step 3 to cover this long edge. Be sure not to topstitch over the pocket (flip the pocket out of the way when doing the topstitching).

6 Sew a 1½" × 13½" (3.8 × 34.5 cm) strip of Ultrasuede to each short edge of the quilted piece, but do not topstitch them yet.

7 Before topstitching these strips in place, make loops for the metal strap holders with the (2) 1" × 4" (2.5 × 10 cm) strips of Ultrasuede. Fold them in half, and pin 1 to the front middle of each short edge of the carrier (raw edges aligned, with the fold pointing inward toward the center of the carrier). Topstitch the Ultrasuede binding as in Step 3. The stitching will anchor the loops in place.

> **Tip**
> If your holders do not have openings, attach the holders before completing the topstitching.

8 For the shoulder strap, fold the 62" (157.5 cm) strip of fabric in half lengthwise, right sides together, and sew a ¼" (6 mm) seam. Turn the tube right-side out and press with the seam in the middle. Topstitch a ½" (1.3 cm) strip of Ultrasuede down the middle of the strip if desired.

9 Follow the manufacturer's instructions to string the shoulder strap through the loops of the slide buckle.

10 Make covered buttons according to the manufacturer's instructions (or use standard buttons). Space the buttons evenly on the front of the carrier (the pocket should be along this edge, but on the interior), about 1½" (3.8 cm) from the edge.

11 On the opposite side of the carrier, determine where to place the elastic ponytail holder loops. Pin the loops to the interior so they extend ½" (1.3 cm) beyond the edge, and sew through the middle of the loops several times to anchor them in place.

Visit **VIVIKA HANSEN DENEGRE** online at vdenegrequilts.blogspot.com.

36 MODERN SEWING PROJECTS

Plastic Bag Dispenser
by Ayumi Takahashi

Pretty patchwork turns a practical plastic bag dispenser into a charming kitchen accessory. This clever stash-busting project has a drawstring cord for hanging and an elastic opening for retrieving bags.

Fabric
- 7 different fabric scraps, each measuring at least 11" × 6" (28 × 15 cm) for patchwork panel (shown: 1 solid and 6 different prints)
- 5" × 18¼" (12.5 × 46.5 cm) piece of linen for shell top
- 18¼" × 12¼" (46.5 × 31 cm) piece of cotton print for lining
- 4¼" × 18¼" (11 × 46.5 cm) piece of cotton print for shell bottom
- 18¼" × 12¼" (46.5 × 31 cm) piece of lightweight fusible interfacing
- Sewing thread to contrast with patchwork panel fabrics
- Sewing thread to coordinate with patchwork panel fabrics
- 5½" (14 cm) of ⅜" (1 cm) wide twill tape
- ½ yd (45.5 cm) of narrow cord (shown: ⅛" [3 mm] diameter)
- 4" (10 cm) of ¼" (6 mm) wide elastic
- Serger (optional)
- Safety pin (optional)

Finished Size
About 11" (28 cm) long × 6" (15 cm) wide.

notes
* All seam allowances are ¼" (6 mm) unless otherwise indicated.
* For explanations of terms and techniques, see Sewing Basics.

Cut Fabric
1 Cut out fifty-four 2½" (6.5 cm) squares from the 7 different patchwork panel fabrics.

Create Patchwork Panel
2 On a flat surface, organize the fabric squares in a grid, 9 squares wide and 6 squares high. Arrange the squares so there is plenty of variety and remember that the first and last rows will be sewn together in the finished project. Beginning with the column of 6 squares on the left, sew the patches into 9 strips of 6 squares each. Press the seams in the first and other odd-numbered strips up and press the even-numbered strips' seams down.

3 Sew the strips together, matching the seams, with the seam allowances pressed in opposite directions to reduce bulk and create a better match (pressed in the previous step). Press the new seams to one side. Following the manufacturer's instructions, fuse the interfacing to the wrong side of the patchwork panel.

4 Set the machine for a zigzag stitch about 4.0 mm wide and 1.6 mm long and thread the machine with the contrasting sewing thread. Topstitch along the patchwork seam lines, centering the zigzag stitch on the seam line.

5 Fold the twill tape in half widthwise and lay it on the upper edge of the patchwork panel, right sides together, 1" (2.5 cm) from the side edge. Position the ends of the twill tape side by side. Baste the twill tape to the patchwork ⅛" (3 mm) from the raw edges (this will be the hanging loop).

Assemble Bag

6 Place the 5" × 18¼" (12.5 × 46.5 cm) linen piece (shell top) on the patchwork panel right sides together and then lay the cotton lining fabric with its right-side down on top of the patchwork panel (the shell top will be sandwiched between the layers). Match the raw edges and stitch together along the patchwork panel's top long edge, catching the twill tape ends in the seam.

7 Lift up the cotton lining and place the 5" × 18¼" (12.5 × 46.5 cm) cotton piece (shell bottom) on the patchwork panel (on the opposite side from the shell top) right sides together and then replace the cotton lining. Match the raw edges and stitch together along the patchwork panel's bottom long edge.

8 Reaching in through an open side of the patchwork panel, turn the dispenser right-side out. The patchwork panel and lining will be wrong sides together, with the top and bottom panels extending outward from the patchwork. Press the top and bottom seams.

9 Use a serger or zigzag stitch to finish the raw side edges of the dispenser. Fold the assembled unit in half lengthwise with right sides together (patchwork panel will be inside, cotton lining fabric will be outside).

10 Align the raw edges and sew the side seam, leaving 2" (5 cm) at both the bottom and the top unstitched. Press the seam open, continuing to press the seam allowances to the wrong side all the way to the top and bottom edges.

11 Turn the bag right-side out and fold the top (linen) and bottom (cotton print) panels into the bag along the seam lines. Leave the twill tape loop extended upward from the patchwork panel. Edgestitch along both the top and the bottom seams, through all layers.

Make Drawstring

12 Fold the top and bottom panels back into position above and below the patchwork. Press ½" (1.3 cm) to the wrong side at the upper edge of the linen panel, then fold and press an additional ½" (1.3 cm) to the wrong side to make a casing for a cord at the top of the bag.

13 Sew very close to the first fold. The pressed seam allowances will make openings where a cord can be inserted at the side seam.

14 Insert the cord through the casing and make knots at the ends of the cord. If necessary, attach a safety pin to one end of the cord, insert it into the casing, and work it along with your fingers until it pops out the other side.

Finish Bottom

15 Repeat Steps 12 and 13 at the bottom of the bag to make a casing for the elastic.

16 Insert the elastic into the casing, using a safety pin as in Step 14, if necessary. As a safety precaution, pin the trailing end of the elastic to the outside of the dispenser so it isn't pulled into the casing as you thread the elastic. Pull both ends of the elastic out, away from the casing, and overlap them ½" (1.3 cm). Join the elastic ends by sewing back and forth through the overlapped area. Work the join into the casing so it doesn't show.

17 Now, fill the dispenser with plastic bags, pull the top cord to close, and tie a pretty bow. Hang the dispenser from the twill tape loop.

Pull the bags through the bottom opening to dispense.

AYUMI TAKAHASHI shares her craft projects and easy sewing tutorials on her blog, *Pink Penguin*, at ayumills.blogspot.com.

Materials

— 3 fabric scraps for the stripes, 1" × 4½" (2.5 × 11.5 cm) strip each

— Main fabric for the front and back, 4½" × 12" (11.5 × 30.5 cm) piece

— Fabric for the lining, 2 pieces 4½" × 6½" (11.5 × 16.5 cm) each

— Fusible fleece, 2 pieces 4½" × 6½" (11.5 × 16.5 cm) each

— ⅛" (3 mm) skinny elastic, 3"–4" (7.5–10 cm) length

— Button

Finished Size
4" × 6" (10 × 15 cm)

note

✱ Use ¼" (6 mm) seam allowances throughout.

Directions

1 Subcut the 4½" × 12" (11.5 × 30.5 cm) piece of main fabric along the long side to make 1 rectangle 2" × 4½" (5 × 11.5 cm), 1 rectangle 3½" × 4½" (9 × 11.5 cm), and 1 rectangle 4½" × 6½" (11.5 × 16.5 cm).

2 Arrange the 2" × 4½" (5 × 11.5 cm) piece of main fabric, the (3) 1" × 4½" (2.5 × 11.5 cm) scrap strips, and the 3½" × 4½" (9 × 11.5 cm) piece of main fabric as illustrated in **figure 1**. Sew the strips together. Your sewn piece should measure the same as the remaining piece of main fabric (the back): 4½" × 6½" (11.5 × 16.5 cm).

3 Following the manufacturer's instructions, iron a piece of fusible fleece to the wrong side of each of these 2 pieces (the pieced front and the back fabric).

4 Quilt the pieced front. I stitched 4 lines of quilting, spaced ¼" (6 mm) apart, both above and below the patchwork section. Quilt the back piece with 6 lines, spaced ¼" (6 mm) apart, starting approximately 1⅝" (4 cm) from the top edge.

5 Place the front and back pieces right sides together. Backstitching at the beginning and end, sew around the sides and bottom, leaving the top open.

6 Place the lining pieces right sides together. Backstitching at the beginning and end, sew around the sides and bottom, leaving a 3"

Cell Phone CASE

by Mary Claire Goodwin

My cell phone has been living in my purse for about a year now, with pens, lip gloss, loose change, and keys. After countless scratches, smudges, and general dustiness, I decided enough was enough. I created a cozy padded case that offers extra protection for any smartphone, or even a small digital camera.

CELL PHONE CASE **39**

(7.5 cm) opening on 1 side (backstitch on either side of the opening). Leave the top open. Clip the corners and turn the lining right-side out.

7 Measure a length of elastic that will loop and fold over the front of the case, easily slipping over your chosen button. Don't forget to include the seam allowance in the measurement.

> **Tip**
> If you don't have elastic on hand or want to use a fun color, try using a ponytail holder.

8 Slip the lining into the case exterior so the right sides are together. Match the top edges and the side seams; pin to secure. Loop your elastic in half and place it loop side down (raw ends up) in between the lining and the back (the side with no patchwork). Align the elastic ends with the fabric raw edges, and center the elastic before pinning it in place. Stitch around the top edge, backstitching as you pass over the elastic.

9 Clip the corners. Pull the lining out of the case exterior, and then pull the case exterior through the opening in the lining. Gently push out the corners and press if desired. Turn the seam allowance of the lining opening to the inside and press; topstitch the opening closed. Insert the lining into the case.

10 Press along the top edge and pin. Topstitch ⅛" (3 mm) around the top edge.

11 Attach the button to the center front of the case where it best fits your elastic loop.

MARY CLAIRE GOODWIN blogs at splendorfallsmc.blogspot.com.

FIGURE 1

40 MODERN SEWING PROJECTS

Materials

— Lightweight canvas or twill, 11½" × 1¾" (29 × 4.5 cm) strip

— Accent fabric, 11½" × 1½" (29 × 3.8 cm) strip

— Swivel clasp (I used the 1" [2.5 cm] silver and ¾" [2 cm] gold Exclusively You Swivel Clasps by Leisure Arts.)

— Zipper foot

Directions

1. Cut an 11½" × 1¾" (29 × 4.5 cm) strip from the canvas or twill.

2. Cut an 11½" × 1½" (29 × 3.8 cm) strip from the accent fabric.

3. Fold in the long edges of the canvas/twill strip so that they meet in the middle on the wrong side of the fabric. Press the strip to secure the fold. Repeat with the accent fabric.

4. Lay the accent strip on top of the canvas strip, wrong sides facing, so there is a small amount of canvas showing on either side of the accent strip. (The raw edges will be between the strips.) Pin the strips together to hold them in place.

5. Slide the swivel clip onto the pinned strips.

6. Bring the short raw edges of the canvas/twill strip together with their right sides facing, unfolding the pressed edges. (You may need to remove some pins in order to do this). Sew the short edges together with a ¼" (6 mm) seam. Repeat for the short raw edges of the accent fabric.

7. Press the seam allowances just sewn (for the short edges of the canvas and accent fabric) in opposite directions. Fold in the previously pressed lengthwise edges, line up the short edge seams, and pin the strips together a couple more times.

8. Starting at the short seam, edgestitch all the way around 1 long edge of the accent strip, removing the pins as you go. Backstitch at the end. Repeat on the other side.

9. Position your swivel clasp against the short edge seam, folding the fabric back so that the seam faces in toward the clasp. You may want to press this seam to flatten it and help it lie better.

10. Use your zipper foot to stitch across the fabric, as close as possible to the clasp. I do this several times for reinforcement. Be sure to do this last step slowly and carefully.

Put your keys on the clasp and go!

Sweet & Simple
KEY FOB

by Corinnea Martindale

These key fobs are a sweet and simple gift that can be made in less than 15 minutes. The only special ingredient required is a swivel clasp.

Visit **CORINNEA MARTINDALE** online at corinneas-chaos.blogspot.com.

> **Tip**
>
> If you do not want to make buttonholes, no problem! Simply stitch two pieces of Velcro where a button and buttonhole would meet, or use sew-on snap fasteners. You can still stitch a button on the cuff for show. It also makes it easy to take the cuff on and off!

Materials
- Small piece of heavyweight interfacing
- Assorted fabric scraps
- Spray basting glue
- Lightweight piece of fabric for lining
- Pencil for marking
- Buttons (Cover your own or use vintage buttons.)

Optional
- Embellishments (ribbons, silk threads, beads)
- Walking foot attachment
- Buttonhole foot
- Small piece of Velcro or sew-on snap fasteners

Directions

1. For simple 1- or 2-button cuffs, measure loosely/comfortably around your wrist, and add approximately 1½" (3.8 cm) to the measurement.

2. Decide on your cuff width and cut out a long piece of heavyweight interfacing using these measurements.

3. Stitch your fabric scraps together, making enough to cover the interfacing. You could have just 2 or 3 large chunky fabric pieces, or lots of tiny pieces making a rainbow of stripes.

4. Spray baste the back of the interfacing and stick it to the back of the patchwork fabric. Trim off any excess fabric.

5. Spray baste the backing fabric to the other side of the interfacing. Make sure the cuff fits around your wrist comfortably.

6. Satin-stitch around the edge of the entire cuff.

7. Measure about ½" (1.3 cm) in from 1 end of the cuff and mark the center with a pencil. If you are making a thicker cuff, you might choose to have 2 buttons. In this case mark accordingly.

8. Line up the pencil marks with the buttonhole foot and make a buttonhole.

9. Stitch the button onto the other end and check the fit around your wrist.

10. Using embroidery thread, embellish with decorative stitches, or stitch on seed beads. Be creative!

Patchwork Fabric Cuffs

by Lucie Summers

Whatever your style, minimalist or bohemian, these quick, fun cuffs are sure to be noticed! Try them with a few simple utility fabrics like denim and linen, or go to town with crazy prints and embroidered embellishment.

Find more from **LUCIE SUMMERS** at summersville.etsy.com.

Sewing Basics
A quick reference guide to basic tools, techniques, and terms

For the projects in this issue (unless otherwise indicated):

* When piecing: Use ¼" (6 mm) seam allowances. Stitch with the right sides together. After stitching a seam, press it to set the seam; then open the fabrics and press the seam allowance toward the darker fabric.
* Yardages are based upon 44" (112 cm) wide fabric.

Sewing Kit

The following items are essential for your sewing kit. Make sure you have these tools on hand before starting any of the projects:

* **ACRYLIC RULER** This is a clear flat ruler, with a measuring grid at least 2" × 18" (5 × 45.5 cm). A rigid acrylic (quilter's) ruler should be used when working with a rotary cutter. You should have a variety of rulers in different shapes and sizes.
* **BATTING** 100% cotton, 100% wool, plus bamboo, silk, and blends.
* **BONE FOLDER** Allows you to make non-permanent creases in fabric, paper, and other materials.
* **CRAFT SCISSORS** To use when cutting out paper patterns.
* **EMBROIDERY SCISSORS** These small scissors are used to trim off threads, clip corners, and do other intricate cutting work.
* **FABRIC** Commercial prints, hand-dyes, cottons, upholstery, silks, wools; the greater the variety of types, colors, designs, and textures, the better.
* **FABRIC MARKING PENS/PENCILS + TAILOR'S CHALK** Available in several colors for use on light and dark fabrics; use to trace patterns and pattern markings onto your fabric. Tailor's chalk is available in triangular pieces, rollers, and pencils. Some forms (such as powdered) can simply be brushed away; refer to the manufacturer's instructions for the recommended removal method for your chosen marking tool.
* **FREE-MOTION OR DARNING FOOT** Used to free-motion quilt.
* **FUSIBLE WEB** Used to fuse fabrics together. There are a variety of products on the market.
* **GLUE** Glue stick, fabric glue, and all-purpose glue.
* **HANDSEWING + EMBROIDERY NEEDLES** Keep an assortment of sewing and embroidery needles in different sizes, from fine to sturdy.
* **IRON, IRONING BOARD + PRESS CLOTHS** An iron is an essential tool when sewing. Use cotton muslin or silk organza as a press cloth to protect delicate fabric surfaces from direct heat. Use a Teflon sheet or parchment paper to protect your iron and ironing board when working with fusible web.
* **MEASURING TAPE** Make sure it's at least 60" (152.5 cm) long and retractable.
* **NEEDLE THREADER** An inexpensive aid to make threading the eye of the needle super fast.
* **PINKING SHEARS** These scissors with notched teeth leave a zigzag edge on the cut cloth to prevent fraying.
* **POINT TURNER** A blunt, pointed tool that helps push out the corners of a project and/or smooth seams. A knitting needle or chopstick may also be used.
* **ROTARY CUTTER + SELF-HEALING MAT** Useful for cutting out fabric quickly. Always use a mat to protect the blade and your work surface (a rigid acrylic ruler should be used with a rotary cutter to make straight cuts).
* **SAFTEY PINS** Always have a bunch on hand.
* **SCISSORS** Heavy-duty shears reserved for fabric only; a pair of small, sharp embroidery scissors; thread snips; a pair of all-purpose scissors; pinking shears.
* **SEAM RIPPER** Handy for quickly ripping out stitches.
* **SEWING MACHINE** With free-motion capabilities.
* **STRAIGHT PINS + PINCUSHION** Always keep lots of pins nearby.
* **TEMPLATE SUPPLIES** Keep freezer paper or other large paper (such as parchment paper) on hand for tracing the templates you intend to use. Regular office paper may be used for templates that will fit. You should also have card stock or plastic if you wish to make permanent templates that can be reused.
* **THIMBLE** Your fingers and thumbs will thank you.
* **THREAD** All types, including hand and machine thread for stitching and quilting; variegated; metallic; 100% cotton; monofilament.
* **ZIPPER FOOT** An accessory foot for your machine with a narrow profile that can be positioned to sew close to the zipper teeth. A zipper foot is adjustable so the foot can be moved to either side of the needle.

Glossary of Sewing Terms and Techniques

BACKSTITCH Stitching in reverse for a short distance at the beginning and end of a seam line to secure the stitches. Most machines have a button or knob for this function (also called backtack).

BASTING Using long, loose stitches to hold something in place temporarily. To baste by machine, use the longest straight stitch length available on your machine. To baste by hand, use stitches at least ¼" (6 mm) long. Use a contrasting thread to make the stitches easier to spot for removal.

BIAS The direction across a fabric that is located at a 45-degree angle from the lengthwise or crosswise grain. The bias has high stretch and a very fluid drape.

BIAS TAPE Made from fabric strips cut on a 45-degree angle to the grainline, the bias cut creates an edging fabric that will stretch to enclose smooth or curved edges. You can buy bias tape ready-made or make your own.

CLIPPING CURVES Involves cutting tiny slits or triangles into the seam allowance of curved edges so the seam will lie flat when turned right-side out. Cut slits along concave curves and triangles (with points toward the seam line) along a convex curve. Be careful not to clip into the stitches.

CLIP THE CORNERS Clipping the corners of a project reduces bulk and allows for crisper corners in the finished project. To clip a corner, cut off a triangle-shaped piece of fabric across the seam allowances at the corner. Cut close to the seam line but be careful not to cut through the stitches.

DART This stitched triangular fold is used to give shape and form to the fabric to fit body curves.

EDGESTITCH A row of topstitching placed very close (1/16"–1/8" [2–3 mm]) to an edge or an existing seam line.

FABRIC GRAIN The grain is created in a woven fabric by the threads that travel lengthwise and crosswise. The lengthwise grain runs parallel to the selvedges; the crosswise grain should always be perpendicular to the lengthwise threads. If the grains aren't completely straight and perpendicular, grasp the fabric at diagonally opposite corners and pull gently to restore the grain. In knit fabrics, the lengthwise grain runs along the wales (ribs), parallel to the selvedges, with the crosswise grain running along the courses (perpendicular to the wales).

FINGER-PRESS Pressing a fold or crease with your fingers as opposed to using an iron.

FUSSY-CUT Cutting a specific motif from a commercial or hand-printed fabric. Generally used to center a motif in a patchwork pattern or to feature a specific motif in an appliqué design. Use a clear acrylic ruler or template plastic to isolate the selected motif and ensure that it will fit within the desired size, including seam allowances.

GRAINLINE A pattern marking showing the direction of the grain. Make sure the grainline marked on the pattern runs parallel to the lengthwise grain of your fabric, unless the grainline is specifically marked as crosswise or bias.

INTERFACING Material used to stabilize or reinforce fabrics. Fusible interfacing has an adhesive coating on one side that adheres to fabric when ironed.

LINING The inner fabric of a garment or bag, used to create a finished interior that covers the raw edges of the seams.

MITER Joining a seam or fold at an angle that bisects the project corner. Most common is a 45-degree angle, like a picture frame, but shapes other than squares or rectangles will have miters with different angles.

OVERCAST STITCH A machine stitch that wraps around the fabric raw edge to finish edges and prevent unraveling. Some sewing machines have several overcast stitch options; consult your sewing machine manual for information on stitch settings and the appropriate presser foot for the chosen stitch (often the standard presser foot can be used). A zigzag stitch can be used as an alternative to finish raw edges if your machine doesn't have an overcast stitch function.

PRESHRINK Many fabrics shrink when washed; you need to wash, dry, and press all your fabric before you start to sew, following the suggested cleaning method marked on the fabric bolt (keep in mind that the appropriate cleaning method may not be machine washing). Don't skip this step!

RIGHT SIDE The front side, or the side that should be on the outside of a finished garment. On a print fabric, the print will be stronger on the right side of the fabric.

RIGHT SIDES TOGETHER The right sides of two fabric layers should be facing each other.

SATIN STITCH (MACHINE) This is a smooth, completely filled column of zigzag stitches achieved by setting the stitch length short enough for complete coverage but long enough to prevent bunching and thread buildup.

SEAM ALLOWANCE The amount of fabric between the raw edge and the seam.

SELVEDGE This is the tightly woven border on the lengthwise edges of woven fabric and the finished lengthwise edges of knit fabric.

SQUARING UP After you have pieced together a fabric block or section, check to make sure the edges are straight and the measurements are correct. Use a rotary cutter and an acrylic ruler to trim the block if necessary.

STITCH IN THE DITCH Lay the quilt sandwich right-side up under the presser foot and sew along the seam line "ditch." The stitches will fall between the two fabric pieces and disappear into the seam.

TOPSTITCH Used to hold pieces firmly in place and/or to add a decorative effect, a topstitch is simply a stitch that can be seen on the outside of the garment or piece. To topstitch, make a line of stitching on the outside (right side) of the piece, usually a set distance from an existing seam.

UNDERSTITCHING A line of stitches placed on a facing (or lining), very near the facing/garment seam. Understitching is used to hold the seam allowances and facing together and to prevent the facing from rolling toward the outside of the garment.

WRONG SIDE The wrong side of the fabric is the underside, or the side that should be on the inside of a finished garment. On a print fabric, the print will be lighter or less obvious on the wrong side of the fabric.

Stitch Glossary

Backstitch
Working from right to left, bring the needle up at **1** and insert behind the starting point at **2**. Bring the needle up at **3**, repeat by inserting at **1** and bringing the needle up at a point that is a stitch length beyond **3**.

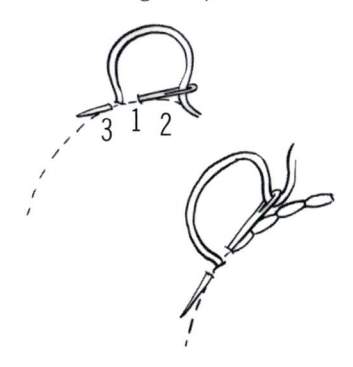

Basting Stitch
Using the longest straight stitch length on your machine, baste to temporarily hold fabric layers and seams in position for final stitching. It can also be done by hand. When basting, use a contrasting thread to make it easier to spot when you're taking it out.

Blanket Stitch
Working from left to right, bring the needle up at **1** and insert at **2**. Bring the needle back up at **3** and over the working thread. Repeat by making the next stitch in the same manner, keeping the spacing even.

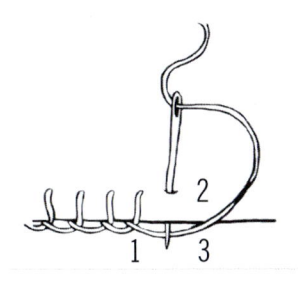

Blindstitch/Blind-Hem Stitch
Used mainly for hemming fabrics where an inconspicuous hem is difficult to achieve (this stitch is also useful for securing binding on the wrong side). Fold the hem edge back about ¼" (6 mm). Take a small stitch in the garment, picking up only a few threads of the fabric, then take the next stitch ¼" (6 mm) ahead in the hem. Continue, alternating stitches between the hem and the garment (if using for a non-hemming application, simply alternate stitches between the two fabric edges being joined).

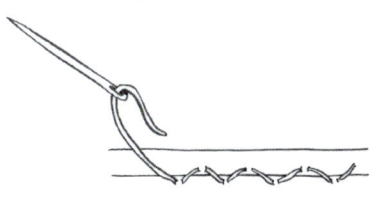

Chain Stitch
Working from top to bottom, bring the needle up at and reinsert at **1** to create a loop; do not pull the thread taut. Bring the needle back up at **2**, keeping the needle above the loop and gently pulling the needle toward you to tighten the loop flush to the fabric.

Repeat by inserting the needle at **2** to form a loop and bring the needle up at **3**. Tack the last loop down with a straight stitch.

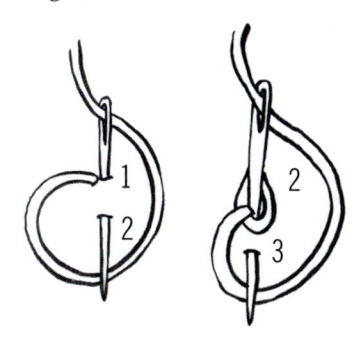

Straight Stitch + Running Stitch
Working from right to left, make a straight stitch by bringing the needle up and insert at **1**, ⅛"–¼" (3–6 mm) from the starting point. To make a line of running stitches (a row of straight stitches worked one after the other), bring the needle up at **2** and repeat.

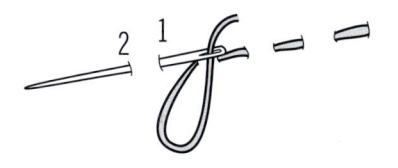

French Knot
Bring the needle up at **1** and hold the thread taut above the fabric. Point the needle toward your fingers and move the needle in a circular motion to wrap the thread around the needle once or twice. Insert the needle near **1** and hold the thread taut near the knot as you pull the needle and thread through the knot and the fabric to complete.

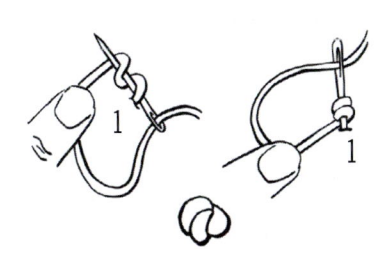

SEWING BASICS **45**

Couching

Working from right to left, use one thread, known as the couching or working thread, to tack down one or more strands of fiber, known as the couched fibers. Bring the working thread up at **1** and insert at **2**, over the fibers to tack them down, bringing the needle back up at **3**. The fibers are now encircled by the couching thread. Repeat to couch the desired length of fiber(s). This stitch may also be worked from left to right, and the spacing between the couching threads may vary for different design effects.

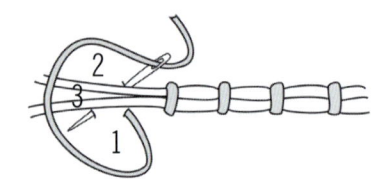

Cross-Stitch

Working from right to left, bring the needle up at **1**, insert at **2**, then bring the needle back up at **3**. Finish by inserting the needle at **4**. Repeat for the desired number of stitches.

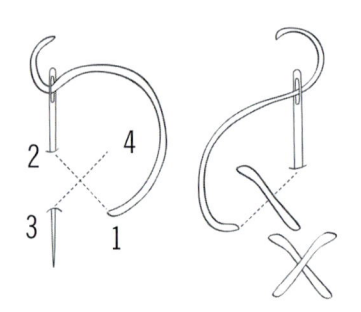

Whipstitch

Bring the needle up at **1**, insert at **2**, and bring up at **3**. These quick stitches do not have to be very tight or close together.

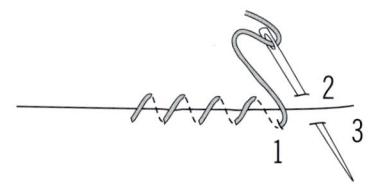

Standard Hand-Appliqué Stitch

Cut a length of thread 12"–18" (30.5–45.5 cm). Thread the newly cut end through the eye of the needle, pull this end through, and knot it. Use this technique to thread the needle and knot the thread to help keep the thread's "twist" intact and to reduce knotting. Beginning at the straightest edge of the appliqué and working from right to left, bring the needle up from the underside, through the background fabric and the very edge of the appliqué at **1**, catching only a few threads of the appliqué fabric. Pull the thread taut, then insert the needle into the background fabric at **2**, as close as possible to **1**. Bring the needle up through the background fabric at **3**, ⅛" (3 mm) beyond **2**. Continue in this manner, keeping the thread taut (do not pull it so tight that the fabric puckers) to keep the stitching as invisible as possible.

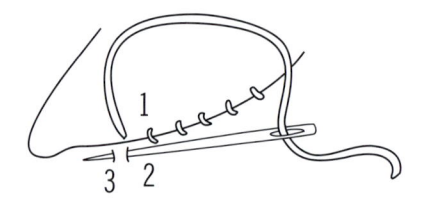

Slip Stitch

Working from right to left, join two pieces of fabric by taking a ¹⁄₁₆"–¼" (2–6 mm) long stitch into the folded edge of one piece of fabric and bringing the needle out. Insert the needle into the folded edge of the other piece of fabric, directly across from the point where the thread emerged from the previous stitch. Repeat by inserting the needle into the first piece of fabric. The thread will be almost entirely hidden inside the folds of the fabrics.

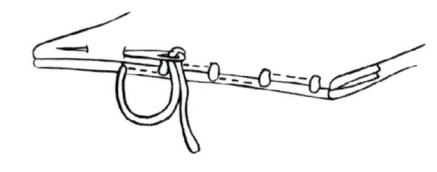

Create Binding

Cutting Straight Strips

Cut strips on the crosswise grain, from selvedge to selvedge. Use a rotary cutter and straightedge to obtain a straight cut. Remove the selvedges and join the strips with diagonal seams (see instructions at right).

Cutting Bias Strips

Fold one cut end of the fabric to meet one selvedge, forming a fold at a 45-degree angle to the selvedge (**1**). With the fabric placed on a self-healing mat, cut off the fold with a rotary cutter, using a straightedge as a guide to make a straight cut. With the straightedge and rotary cutter, cut strips to the appropriate width (**2**). Join the strips with diagonal seams.

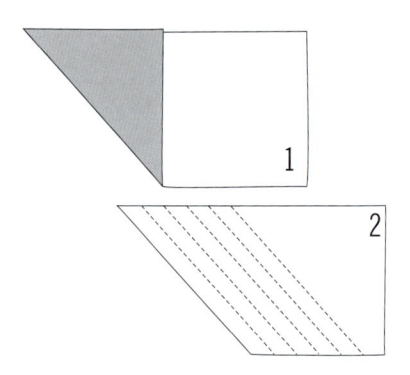

Binding with Mitered Corners

Decide whether you will use a Double-fold Binding (option A at right) or a Double-layer Binding (option B at right). *If using double-layer binding follow the alternate italicized instructions in parenthesis.*

Open the binding and press ½" (1.3 cm) to the wrong side at one short end *(refold the binding at the center crease and proceed)*. Starting with the folded-under end of the binding, place it near the center of the first edge of the project to be bound, matching the raw edges, and pin in place. Begin sewing near the center of one edge of the project, along the first crease *(at the appropriate distance from the raw edge)*, leaving several inches of the binding fabric free at the beginning. Stop sewing ¼" (6 mm) before

46 MODERN SEWING PROJECTS

reaching the corner, backstitch, and cut the threads. Rotate the project 90 degrees to position it for sewing the next side. Fold the binding fabric up, away from the project, at a 45-degree angle (**1**), then fold it back down along the project raw edge (**2**). This forms a miter at the corner. Stitch the second side, beginning at the project raw edge (**2**) and ending ¼" (6 mm) from the next corner, as before.

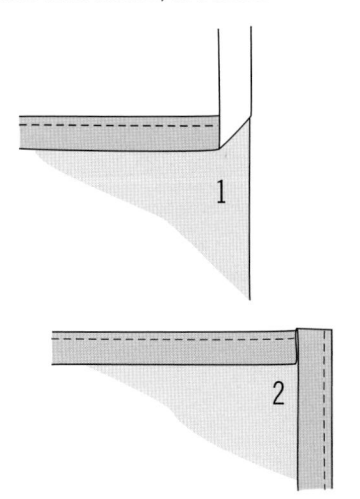

Continue as established until you have completed the last corner. Continue stitching until you are a few inches from the beginning edge of the binding fabric. Overlap the pressed beginning edge of the binding by ½" (1.3 cm) (or overlap more as necessary for security) and trim the working edge to fit. Finish sewing the binding *(opening the center fold and tucking the raw edge inside the pressed end of the binding strip)*. Refold the binding along all the creases and then fold it over the project raw edges to the back, enclosing the raw edges *(there are no creases to worry about with option B)*. The folded edge of the binding strip should just cover the stitches visible on the project back. Slip-stitch or blindstitch the binding in place, tucking in the corners to complete the miters as you go (**3**).

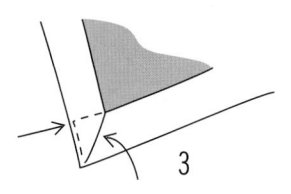

Diagonal Seams for Joining Strips

Lay two strips right sides together, at right angles. The area where the strips overlap forms a square. Sew diagonally across the square as shown above. Trim the excess fabric ¼" (6 mm) away from the seam line and press the seam allowances open. Repeat to join all the strips, forming one long fabric band.

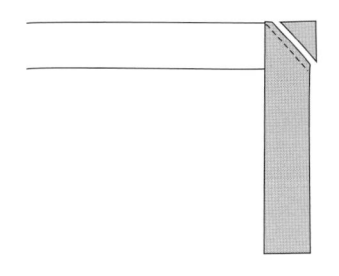

Fold Binding

A. Double-fold Binding

This option will create binding that is similar to packaged double-fold bias tape/binding. Fold the strip in half lengthwise, with wrong sides together; press. Open up the fold and then fold each long edge toward the wrong side, so that the raw edges meet in the middle (**1**). Refold the binding along the existing center crease, enclosing the raw edges (**2**), and press again.

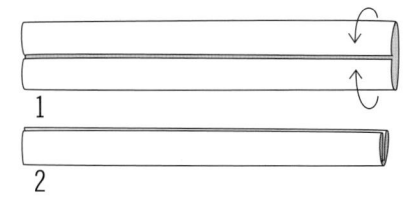

B. Double-layer Binding

This option creates a double-thick binding with only one fold. This binding is often favored by quilters. Fold the strip in half lengthwise with wrong sides together; press.

SEWING BASICS **47**

Find popular patterns for quick and easy projects with these *Craft Tree* publications, brought to you by Interweave.

THESE CRAFT TREE BOOKLETS ONLY $14.99!

Evening Bags
ISBN 978-1-59668-764-6

Everyday Totes
ISBN 978-1-59668-774-5

Fun Home Accessories
ISBN 978-1-59668-769-1

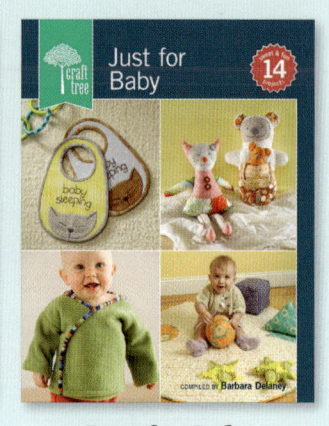

Just for Baby
ISBN 978-1-59668-773-8

Just for Kids
ISBN 978-1-59668-772-1

Modern Sewing Projects
ISBN 978-1-59668-768-4

Notebook Covers
ISBN 978-1-59668-766-0

Patchwork Pillows
ISBN 978-1-59668-767-7

Scarves and Wraps
ISBN 978-1-59668-770-7

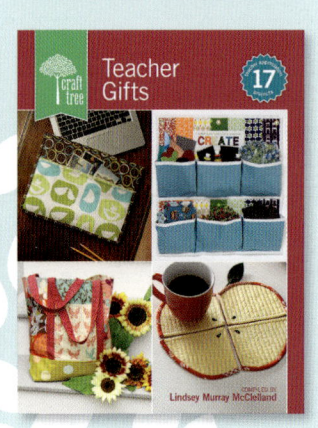

Teacher Gifts
ISBN 978-1-59668-765-3

Travel Accessories
ISBN 978-1-59668-771-4

Visit your favorite retailer or order online at **interweavestore.com**

INTERWEAVE
interweavestore.com